"At Walmart, we believe that our people make the difference. While technology continues to help us make jobs easier, it's our associates who make Walmart special. Now more than ever, we are underscoring the critical role our managers play in communities around the world, and we continue to invest in their growth and development. This welcome research from McKinsey reinforces how critical these investments are for managers in frontline and campus office roles."

—**DONNA MORRIS,** Executive Vice President and Chief People Officer, Walmart

"Delta's success is driven by our ninety thousand people worldwide, and our leaders and managers play a critical role in maintaining that momentum. This book provides practical ideas on how to support midlevel managers and celebrate their important impact."

—**ED BASTIAN,** CEO, Delta Air Lines

"A playbook to unleash the power of your talent, drive strategy execution, and elevate your business performance."

—**MONA MALONE,** Chief Human Resources Officer and Head of People & Culture, BMO Financial Group

"An illuminating and inspiring read on why investing in your people managers matters now more than ever, with actionable insights for leaders navigating the evolution of the workplace and workforce."

—**MICHAEL FRACCARO,** Chief Human Resources Officer, Mastercard

"Middle managers are the key to driving sustained value creation in organizations. *Power to the Middle* demonstrates why and provides business leaders with the tools they need to optimize the performance of these mission-critical people."

—**ERIC KUTSENDA,** cofounder and Managing Partner, Seidler Equity Partners

"New technologies are changing work and working lives. Successful companies make the necessary transitions by engaging their employees at every stage in the process. In this insightful book, the authors highlight the importance of managers in making a success of this engagement and the ongoing transition."

—**SIR CHRIS PISSARIDES,** Nobel Laureate in Economic Sciences; Regius Professor of Economics, London School of Economics; and cofounder and Cochair, Institute for the Future of Work

"Our talent strategy helps us to reach more patients more quickly with life-changing therapies. Middle managers are at the center of this process, and this book helps CEOs understand why and how they should reimagine the role of managers in their organizations."

—**TIM WALBERT,** Chairman, President, and CEO, Horizon Therapeutics

"It's inspiring to read this recognition and celebration of middle managers and to have a guide to their engagement. They are the leaders who hold the keys to deep customer and frontline employee relationships."

—**DAVID BAIADA,** CEO, BAYADA Home Health Care

POWER TO
THE MIDDLE

POWER TO

Why Managers
Hold the Keys
to the Future
of Work

THE MIDDLE

Bill Schaninger | Bryan Hancock | Emily Field

HARVARD BUSINESS REVIEW PRESS
BOSTON, MASSACHUSETTS

Library of Congress Cataloging-in-Publication Data

Names: Schaninger, Bill, 1969– author. | Hancock, Bryan, author. |
    Field, Emily (Writer on Industrial management), author.
Title: Power to the middle : why managers hold the keys to the future of work /
    by Bill Schaninger, Bryan Hancock, and Emily Field.
Description: Boston, Massachusetts : Harvard Business Review Press, [2023] |
    Includes index. |
Identifiers: LCCN 2022060240 (print) | LCCN 2022060241 (ebook)
Subjects: LCSH: Middle managers. | Industrial management. | Success in business.
Classification: LCC HD38.24 .S45 2023 (print) | LCC HD38.24 (ebook) |
    DDC 658.4/3—dc23/eng/20230327
LC record available at https://lccn.loc.gov/2022060240
LC ebook record available at https://lccn.loc.gov/2022060241

ISBN: 978-1-64782-485-3
eISBN: 978-1-64782-486-0

This book is dedicated to middle managers everywhere who are being asked to achieve more with less; who feel a perpetual tug to leave the work they love in pursuit of advancement; and who strive daily to be outstanding leaders of their teams. Thank you for inspiring us to renew our focus on the middle.

CONTENTS

Seeing Managers Differently in a New World of Work

For two and a half years Van, the CEO of a fast-growing tech company, felt himself careening from one crisis to the next. First, the worldwide pandemic seriously disrupted his operations. In particular, the company's abrupt switch to remote work was poorly executed and led to millions in lost business.

During the first phase of the pandemic in 2020, Van felt like he just didn't have control of his widely dispersed workers. As soon as he was able, he ordered them to return to the office for at least three days a week. At a meeting with his middle managers announcing the change, one of them, Tina, noted that three of her team members had moved several hours from the city and would now have a long commute. "People might start looking at places that offer fully remote work," Tina said, and several other department heads nodded in agreement. Van acknowledged their concerns, but stuck to his position that it was more important for employees to gather regularly at the office.

Several months later, just as Tina had anticipated, Van was confronted by a wave of resignations. Some of his top engineers started leaving for other companies, especially, he noted with chagrin, his chief competitor.

Van responded by dramatically increasing his engineers' salaries. But still, the revolving door kept turning. (Van would have swallowed his pride and asked Tina for advice at this point, but, feeling underappreciated, she had been one of those to take an offer at another company.)

Then came the next blow: In 2022, the stock market tumbled and at the same time demand for his company's services plummeted. Now Van's company was in major financial trouble, and he felt he had no choice but to reduce head count. An email went out to 10 percent of his employees informing them that they were losing their jobs. Van felt terrible to see so many talented people leave, but in these unprecedented times, what choice did he have?

And yet he couldn't help following developments at his chief competitor, run by Claire, a former classmate of his at Stanford. Claire's company, as far as he knew, had not laid off *any* employees.

Van just didn't understand it. They were similar companies, offering similar services, and about the same size. What was it about Claire's company that enabled it to emerge relatively unscathed from an economic crisis?

The answer: Unlike most of her peers, Claire had invested in her middle managers.

A year before the pandemic hit, Claire realized that her middle management layer was seriously untrained and underdeveloped, and that this was affecting employee performance and ultimately the company's bottom line. So she put a pause on most new projects and devoted a large share of her time, money, and energy into hiring, promoting, and training managers. Some of the people on her leadership team questioned the move, worried that it would slow the company's release of new services in a competitive and cutting-edge industry.

But Claire held firm, and her decision proved wise when the pandemic shook the world. Of course, Claire had not known that this particular crisis would occur, but she had built an infrastructure of managers who were now equipped to deal with the unexpected in its myriad forms.

And this they did. They worked with their tech experts to quickly set up a reliable and highly collaborative remote work operation. When employees had to miss work because of Covid-19, managers came up with creative ways to reassign the work. And above all, managers made sure to show care and compassion for the people who worked for them—both as employees and as human beings who were facing an incredibly stressful time.

Like Van, Claire initially wanted to require employees to return to the office at least a few days a week. She too held a meeting with her middle managers about the issue. But instead of announcing a top-down change in policy, she opened the floor to her middle managers and asked them what they thought.

"I think my team members will be okay with coming in a few days a week as long as there are good reasons for them to be in the office, and I can work on that," said Ivan.

"Wow, I can't see this going over very well with most of my team," said James. "Almost all of them say they're more productive working remotely. We've got a good rhythm going, and I'd hate to ruin that."

"I can tell you right now, three of my engineers would walk out the door if they had to start coming in," said Rosa, always the blunt one of the group.

Each of her managers had a different response to the remote work conundrum. And that's when Claire realized that she needed to trust each of her managers to decide when their employees needed to be in the office, and when they could work from home, recognizing that this would vary from department to department.

All these actions caused employees at Claire's firm to feel loyal to their managers—and to stay at the company. As a result, attrition wasn't as much of an issue when "the Great Resignation" took hold. Good word of mouth and positive reviews on sites like Glassdoor kept the applications coming.

Then the economic downturn arrived. At first Claire was afraid she would need to lay off some of her employees. But with the help of her managers, she was able to redeploy workers in the hardest-hit areas to departments where demand was still high. Yes, her company took a financial hit, but it wasn't nearly as pronounced as the one Van experienced.

When Van started his company, he had not had a middle management layer at all. As the company grew he realized that if he didn't have managers the company would descend into chaos. But most of his managers came from the front line without any training in people management. And so when Covid-19 came on the scene, they were ill prepared for the rapid-fire problems it presented.

Then, when the downturn hit, Van had so many fires to put out that he didn't have time to thoughtfully redeploy his workers, and his managers weren't trained to do that work. So Van simply whacked from the bottom to cut costs. That's when he started to realize that better-trained middle managers would have been a huge advantage.

Claire's managers did have that advantage, because of the investment she had made in middle managers several years earlier.

The Mishandling of Managers

A cost-cutting opportunity.

That's the way many organizations have viewed their middle managers over the past thirty years. And now they're paying the price.

That's why the three of us, management consultants at McKinsey, decided to write this book. And we do see the irony in that. Because over the last several decades, consulting companies—focused on efficiency and shareholder value for their clients—often encouraged the very perception that middle managers were a source of high cost and low value.

One of us, Bill, spent the early parts of his career focused on reducing costs and achieving efficiencies for his clients. Reducing middle managers was one means of measuring and improving shareholder value. But as Bill continued to work with global companies, he saw countless real-world examples of middle managers having a significant, positive impact on their organizations, and he began to wonder: How many other types of value—not quite so easy to measure—were lost because of mathematically focused cost-cutting measures?

For Bryan, a crystallizing moment occurred when he learned of a survey that found that more than 40 percent of workers said no one at their organization had asked them how they were doing during the pandemic.[1] This was clearly a middle manager's job, and the fact that it wasn't being done signaled how severely this role has been depleted.

In working with their clients, and in researching the future of work over the last several years, Bill, Bryan, and Emily have seen over and over that the very management layer that has been so severely beaten down is now absolutely vital to achieving organizational success. And most senior leaders still don't realize that.

Like Van, the CEO of the tech firm, they react on the fly to one crisis after the next without realizing that these sudden changes—whatever form they may take—are never going to stop. In order to respond to them both quickly and thoughtfully, we need a strong layer of people managers.

As the very definition and meaning of work undergo seismic changes, our current organizational structures are simply not built to adapt to them. We argue that organizations need to pivot not from the top or the bottom but from the middle in order to thrive.

We wrote this book to puncture the persistent negative stereotypes that surround middle management. We want to encourage organizations to adopt a new mindset and a new model that puts middle managers at the very center of changes in work, the workforce, and the workplace.

Right now the very term "middle manager" is freighted with negativity, connoting as it does a twentieth-century idea of bureaucracy and make-work within a strict organizational hierarchy. Who actually self-identifies as a middle manager anymore, even if they are one? This underrated role—which we define as operating between team leaders/frontline workers and senior executives—is long overdue for a makeover.

We argue that middle managers—uniquely positioned close to the ground, but not *too* close—will be at the forefront of guiding their organizations through a coming period of rapid and complex change. They are an essential link between the front line and the senior leaders who are shaping and guiding strategy.

To meet the demands of the new world of work, though, managers must be allowed to shed their roles as paper pushers, bureaucrats, and rule enforcers, and reinvent themselves as coaches, connectors, navigators, and talent managers. This will be a huge leap for those who now spend most of their time making PowerPoint presentations and defending the status quo.

Many managers could excel at their jobs, but their own bosses deny them the opportunity to make a difference. A recent McKinsey survey found that middle managers are, on average, spending almost three-quarters of their time on tasks other than managing their teams.[2]

Most say talent management isn't seen as a top priority at their organizations. Forty-eight percent say they don't have the time, and over a third say they don't have adequate resources, to actually manage their employees. A substantial share say that organizational bureaucracy (39 percent) and unsustainable work demands (30 percent) are getting in the way of their fulfilling their true potential as leaders.

It's clear that many in the C-suite are giving short shrift to their managers by requiring them to perform individual contributor work (an average of 28 percent of their time) in addition to their other duties. This seriously dilutes their ability to make lasting changes.

To make matters worse, many senior leaders have been conditioned to believe that if middle managers are truly good at managing people, then they should be promoted out of their jobs. In this book, we argue that the smartest executives will do everything in their power to keep their best middle managers exactly where they are, and reward them.

That's right. Don't promote these employees to different roles. Instead, find ways to move managers upward in their current jobs. Many senior leaders still don't realize that good managers—the ones with true people skills—are hard to replace. A job this crucial should not turn over quickly. If they can, senior leaders should pay these managers more and shower them with bonuses, but those are far from the only rewards available. Allow them more flexibility, give them the most desirable assignments, expand their influence or geographic range—whatever is most important to them, as long as they continue doing their important work. When managers shed their roles as administrators and bureaucrats and emerge as true people leaders, their positions become invaluable and invulnerable to displacement.

In the future, we hope more senior leaders will empower their managers to look beyond what has made them successful in the past, and proceed to reimagine their roles. Based on our in-depth experience as consultants at McKinsey, we will tell you stories about managers who have been able to do just that. These include:

- A consumer goods manager who refused to take a promotion into senior leadership because he loved the job he was doing—and who proceeded to help change his company's mindset around recognizing and rewarding middle managers.

- A grocery store manager and an insurance company manager who retrained and redeployed employees whose jobs were about to be replaced by automation.

- A gaming company manager who talked her bosses out of enacting a unilateral return-to-work policy after the pandemic, and helped stop a serious attrition problem in the process.

- A manager of oil drillers who was facing an attrition problem of his own, and who would never have realized the surprising reasons for it if not for an illuminating employee survey.

- An advertising agency manager who took her job as a coach seriously and improved the work of a low performer who had been "promoted" to her department by a manager who didn't want to deal with the issue.

Of course, we haven't just seen the good side of middle management; we've seen the bad and the ugly, too. We'll also tell you some of those stories, including:

- An education company manager who took a promotion to the executive level because that's the way the system works when you're good at what you do—but who loathed her new job and soon resigned.

- A hiring manager who lost a top software-engineering applicant to a competitor because he couldn't fathom that she valued more than just a high salary.

- A tech company with a jaded layer of "permafrost" managers who refused to join in the enthusiasm that frontline workers and senior leaders shared over an innovative new sensor with exciting applications.

- A research institute manager who found the perfect candidate for a very hard-to-fill position—only to be told by human resources that she couldn't hire him.

Through these stories and many others we hope to illustrate how middle managers, more so than any other role, can either impede or unleash an organization's success.

Why Us?

Why are the three of us in particular writing a book about middle management? Because all of us have become convinced, through our experiences at McKinsey, that middle managers hold the key to making work more meaningful, purposeful, interesting, and productive for everyone—including the managers themselves.

Organizations come to us when they're facing big thorny problems that they haven't been able to solve on their own. Maybe they're having trouble melding two cultures after a merger. Or they're facing a huge drop in demand for a legacy product. Or they're confronting a major attrition problem.

The reasons are as individual as the organizations that seek our help. And yet, time and again, we have found that whatever the problem is, true organizational change can only occur with the active involvement of middle managers.

We have frequently observed the effects of a vicious cycle: Without training, trust, and empowerment, managers remain underutilized. At the same time, senior leadership mistakes its own lack of investment in managers as a sign that they are inherently peripheral, or even unnecessary, to success. And yet nothing could be further from the truth.

We have also witnessed that aha moment when executives finally realized that their middle managers were the missing link in achieving their goals. And we all have compelling stories of how they turned that realization into concrete action, yielding tangible business results.

Just three examples among many: Bill helped an entertainment company empower its managers to tailor and fine-tune its hybrid work policies; Bryan helped a fast-growing biotech company build a management layer that hadn't existed before; Emily helped a financial firm become more execution-focused and performance-driven by strengthening the capabilities of its managers. With each new transformation that featured managers in the starring role, we knew we had the makings of a new paradigm—one that was worthy of its own book.

We hope this book will serve as a wake-up call to senior leaders who have failed to give their middle managers the time, tools, and training they so desperately need. We also hope it will serve as a support and guide for the tens of millions of middle managers who work tirelessly to support their teams, sometimes in extremely challenging situations.

A Map of This Book

In part I, "Wasting Our Most Valuable Players," we describe the current state of middle management at most organizations, with managers relating how ineffective and exhausting their work has become, mostly due to unrealistic expectations from senior leaders whose priorities lie elsewhere. And we explain how we got to this point: because executives are still mindlessly following obsolete and misguided practices that have no place in a forward-thinking, constantly shifting workplace.

In part II, "Putting Managers at the Center," we discuss how managers' roles can evolve to better respond to the challenges of the twenty-first century workplace. First, we advise redefining and reframing managers' jobs so that they become the most important and desirable roles in the organization. Then we show how, from this newly imagined vantage point, managers can take the lead to:

- *Rebundle jobs rather than eliminate them.* As automation continues to transform workplaces, senior leaders will turn to their in-house experts—middle managers—to lead realignments. Only they have both the granular knowledge and wide perspective to take apart roles and rebundle them into whole jobs that should be done by humans. And only they can ensure that new and sophisticated interfaces between employees and machines actually run smoothly.

- *Actively recruit and retain workers.* The balance of power in the labor market has shifted, and in many jobs—especially in the skilled professions—it's the workers who hold the reins. People will gravitate to the employers that offer not just competitive salary and benefits, but also a work experience that aligns with their values, purpose, and long-term career goals. The middle manager is the one who is best positioned to outline the employee value proposition to job candidates and then follow through with it on a daily basis with those who are hired.

- *Continuously coach and develop employees.* We show how middle managers can take a more purpose-driven and holistic view of performance management, one that is driven by the cadence of the work and not the calendar. And we show how they can link individual purpose and corporate purpose—while also demonstrating compassion—in a way that lifts their performance even further.

- *Use data to solve problems in a thoughtful way.* As managers work to recruit and retain employees, and improve their performance, they can be trained to rely on data, not just their gut, to make decisions. By using data wisely, and uncovering the biases and blind spots that may well lurk within it, they can elevate both their own and their employees' work.

- *Work productively with human resources to find the best talent and improve performance.* Managers can help HR shift from enforcing rules to challenging them. Because their position allows managers to see when things stop working, they are a critical bulwark against rules that are ineffective, obsolete, or counterproductive. And when it comes to performance, too many managers have ceded this function to the human resource department, which isn't meant to provide the kind of continuous coaching needed to develop individual employees.

- *Strive to connect the work to the people instead of the people to the work.* As work moves steadily away from a hierarchical headquarters model, managers will be central to aligning individual purpose and corporate purpose—and in designing work solutions that both show empathy and also further the company's goals.

At the end of the book, we sum up our insights and provide a playbook that will help senior leaders let go of the command-and-control mindset that has hobbled their managers for so long. Future-forward leaders will share the power with their managers and provide the coaching and training that enables them to thrive.

A word about the stories here: We take the confidentiality of our clients very seriously. At the same time, we wanted to take you deep inside what it's like to be a middle manager in this pivotal era. The best way to do that was to use composite stories, which realistically represent our combined experiences with our clients while still protecting their anonymity.

We think you will recognize the people and situations in these stories, whether you are a leader at your company with middle managers reporting to you, a middle manager yourself, or you are working for a middle manager and experiencing many of the challenges we illustrate. We hope that our depiction of these struggles and successes will inspire you to view the value—and the potential—of middle managers in a whole new way.

PART

I

Wasting Our Most Valuable Players

CHAPTER 1

Why Managers Are So Frustrated

A Neglect of Their Primary Purpose

Renee has a scar from a job she once held as a middle manager.[1]

We're not talking about a psychological scar, although she has a few of those, too. This is a real scar that she sees on the back of her hand every time she works on her computer or sits down to a meal.

The scar is an ever-present reminder of a day in December that Renee knew was going to be bad when she got into her car and drove to the clothing and accessories store that she managed. She just didn't realize how bad.

Renee tried to start the day with a positive attitude because that's what good managers do. And Renee was born to be a manager. She loved anything that involved teamwork. At age twelve, she volunteered to help build the first recycling center in the small southwestern town where she lived. In high school, she played on a new and relatively short-statured volleyball team that was scrappy enough to make it all the way to the state championship.

While working part-time at a mom-and-pop clothing store in college, Renee fell in love with retail. She enjoyed working with her colleagues to help elevate the customer experience. She had worked at several old-line retailers before winding up at the clothing and accessories store, which was a startup. As someone in charge of her own store, she was one common example of a retail middle manager.

The founders of the startup were well-meaning, but the company was growing so quickly that they didn't have time to focus on—or didn't think they needed to invest in—their managers. As a result, their middle managers ended up doing jobs that weren't the best use of their time. Managers were also expected to be on call 24-7, even when they were on vacation.

Senior leaders at the startup looked at their Excel spreadsheets and decided that Renee's store should generate $3 million in sales, but they didn't help her develop a marketing campaign, or strategize with her on how to recruit the best salespeople. She was left to muddle through on her own.

Even with all the obstacles she faced, Renee did her best to look out for her team. But her own manager, Jane at regional headquarters, did not do the same for Renee. Jane didn't check in very often with Renee; she was friendly enough, but her attention was focused on the C-suite. Mainly Jane issued edicts from on high, and Renee was expected to follow them.

When corporate decided to open a holiday pop-up store in a different part of town, Jane told Renee that she would need to oversee the effort and divert several of her employees to the store for most of December. This was during the pandemic, when labor shortages in retail were severe. When Renee said she wouldn't have time to give the pop-up the attention it deserved and that it would leave her own store understaffed during its busiest time, Jane brushed off her concerns. "I know you can make it work," Jane said.

On that day in December, only Renee and one of her team leaders were at her store to deal with a long line of Christmas shoppers who had gathered before the doors opened. A few more employees would come in later, but the remainder were at the pop-up.

Luckily, Renee had a great rapport with her team leader, Larissa, and they both tried to grin and bear it as the day wore on and customers grew progressively more annoyed and impatient while waiting to receive assistance and pay for their purchases. A few customers expressed dramatic disbelief and outrage that the store had run out of gift boxes.

To make matters worse, the store had a monogram machine, and employees including Renee sometimes had to abandon their posts to handle customers' monogramming requests—including one woman who wanted to have fifteen belts and handbags initialed. The customer was understanding when Renee asked her to go for a coffee and come back in a few hours, but her order combined with all the others caused Renee to feel flustered and rushed as she placed yet another purse under the machine.

And that's when it happened: in a moment of distraction, the multiple super-sharp needles of the machine came down on Renee's hand instead of the handbag, branding her to this day. She tried not to yelp too loudly, quickly found a bandage to wrap the wound, and carried on with her monogramming.

Renee didn't bother to call Jane about the situation at the store that day because she knew it would be futile. Jane would just tell her to "deal with it." Renee did find a few minutes to order lunch for her employees. She also checked in with the workers at the pop-up store, who reported that they were bored because it had been empty almost the entire day. Renee had simply not had time to arrange for the marketing that would make people aware of its existence.

Finally, after twelve hours with no breaks, Renee sent her exhausted employees home with her heartfelt thanks, and finished with the remaining monogramming orders. She walked to her car and saw that it was blocked bumper to bumper on both ends so she couldn't get out. She got in, shut the door, sat at the wheel, and sobbed uncontrollably until the car in front of her pulled out. Then she went home and downed two large glasses of wine.

In the following days, the online customer reviews of the store were scathing.

At their next Zoom meeting, Jane mentioned the reviews and the poor sales at the pop-up store. When Renee explained what had happened, Jane nodded her head and said she understood. Still, Renee did not really feel heard, and she did not feel supported. She still felt, in some way, that Jane was saying that all of this was Renee's fault. It was not long after this meeting that Renee decided to quit her job.

Ignoring the Most Important Role

What Renee went through as a middle manager in that job is a microcosm of what many in her position, in all types of industries, are facing every day: a lack of time, a lack of resources, a lack of appreciation, and a lack of agency to perform one of the most important roles—no, *the* most important role—at an organization: managing talent.

We define middle managers as the people who are at least once removed from the front line and at least a layer below the senior leadership. From this pivotal position, a middle manager's job is to bring out the best in their people, and in that way bring out the best in their organizations. They do this best by serving as navigators, connectors, and coaches.

But in most cases senior leaders, failing to realize this, are putting their middle managers to the wrong use. They are using them as a kind of catch-all to do all the tasks that no one else is willing, able, or available to do. As a result, managers are suffering under a host

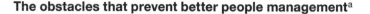

FIGURE 1-1

The obstacles that prevent better people management^a

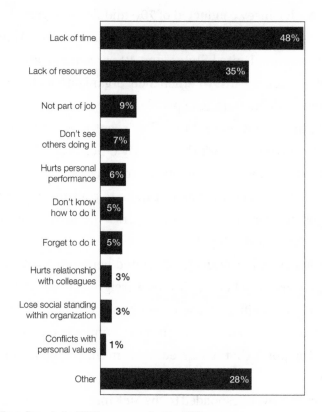

Source: McKinsey Power to the Middle survey results, May 2022.

a. This part of the survey covers only middle managers who spent less than 25 percent of their time on talent and people management.

of burdens and stresses that have stretched them beyond their limits (figure 1-1). And they are being blamed for outcomes that are not their fault.

Think how much better Renee's day would have gone if only she had received more coaching, and been given more time and authority to plan ahead. She could have thoughtfully planned marketing and staffing for the pop-up; ramped up hiring at the main store for the holidays; and considered how to streamline monogramming and other special requests at peak hours. As it was, she was forced to lurch from one crisis to the next.

A survey McKinsey conducted of 700 middle managers shows just how serious the problem is across a range of industries.[2] Almost half of managers in the United States, and 42 percent globally, said they disagreed or were unsure whether their organizations had set them up to be successful managers of people.

Overall, the managers said that they spent more of their time on individual contributor work than on any other type of work. We've seen this with many of our clients. Executives promote someone to a management role and then expect them to continue doing some of their old job, too. Or they expect managers to perform frontline roles to make up for staff shortages.

In Renee's case, her manager expected her to step in and monogram bags. Certainly her employees were grateful for the help, but this was a very inefficient use of her time. Dragooning managers into frontline work became much more common during the pandemic, to the point that it started to seem like standard operating procedure.

The managers who responded to the McKinsey survey also said they were spending an average of nearly 20 percent of their time, or one full workday per week, on administrative work (figure 1-2). And it probably isn't a coincidence that they also felt that the biggest obstacle to their success as people managers was organizational bureaucracy.[3]

Too many organizations have lost sight of the fact that the talent of management—the real energy, creativity, and focus—should be unleashed toward the management of talent. Put another way, the best managers attract and keep the best people. We firmly believe that well-performing individuals in well-structured middle management roles are the secret weapon in the war for talent, a term that McKinsey introduced twenty-five years ago. Now, faced with the perfect storm of automation, hybrid work, economic uncertainty, a scarcity

FIGURE 1-2

How middle managers spend their time

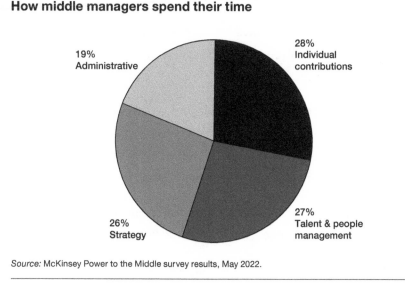

Source: McKinsey Power to the Middle survey results, May 2022.

of skilled workers, and profound shifts in attitudes, whether an organization wins or loses will depend largely on its middle managers.

But right now, many managers are simply not equipped to take on the challenge. That's because the headwinds they face are just too strong. In talking with middle managers like Renee, some common themes emerged:

- Many felt that it was their responsibility to protect their teams from misguided executives. More than one mentioned having to shelter their employees from a toxic leader higher up in the hierarchy. A common thread: Senior leaders just don't understand the details of a task or strategy and too often ask for the impossible.

- Middle managers understand the importance of training—for both their employees and themselves—but often have trouble getting buy-in and budget from senior executives who are focused on the short-term bottom line.

- A word that middle managers used a lot: trust. They want their bosses to trust them to get things done and make changes in their own way, and that's how they gain the trust of their team. But all too often, they don't feel they are receiving that trust from above.

- Some would prefer to stay in their jobs but see no choice but to seek other positions because the reward systems—compensation, equity, bonuses, and promotional opportunities—just aren't in place if they want to grow within their organizations.

- There is a huge psychological strain that goes along with having this job—one that affects both work and home life.

One middle manager, Gavin, who works at a pharmacy, said he feels more like a babysitter than a manager. He's constantly dealing with issues like vacation scheduling, or rushing to find replacements for pharmacists who have called out sick. Or he's handling the complex administrative and compliance issues that surround prescriptions. His phone never lets up, even on evenings and weekends and when he's on vacation. He rarely has time to think about things like how to develop his team leaders and pharmacists, or how to improve profit margins, because he's always rushing to put out the next fire.

By the time he gets home after a long day, Gavin feels completely wrung out, and he barely has any energy for his two young children. He used to be happy-go-lucky kind of guy, he says, but not so much anymore. If things don't change, he can't see himself in the job much longer. He knows of startup pharmacy companies that offer a better work environment, plus stock options, and he's thinking about applying.

"I just don't want that type of negativity in my life," says Gavin. "Why can't I catch a break? That's what it feels like now."

Pressure From Above and Below

A Columbia University study of nearly 22,000 full-time workers found that middle managers and supervisors experience higher levels of anxiety and depression than either executives or frontline workers.[4] This came as a surprise to the researchers, who assumed that the lower a worker's status and power, the more their mental health would suffer.

The researchers cited the pressures of constantly switching between contradictory roles as a big reason for the unexpected findings. These managers commanded higher salaries and (supposedly) possessed higher status and autonomy than their subordinates. But their lower pay and rank compared to executives turned them into a punching bag on both ends. Too often they were forced to give orders based on decisions that were not their own, and then ended up taking the blame when things didn't turn out as planned. In short, they actually had *less* power and control than the people who reported to them, and this caused them to become socially disadvantaged, the study found.

An article in the *Harvard Business Review* titled "Why Being a Middle Manager Is So Exhausting" explains: "In many cases, the norms and expectations associated with being a leader (e.g., assertiveness) are incompatible with the norms and expectations with being a subordinate (e.g., deference). This becomes problematic when one is called upon to play both roles at work because humans are notoriously inefficient when it comes to task switching."[5] This constant vertical task-switching can take an emotional and cognitive toll, the article states, and it can even lead to health problems like heart disease and hypertension.

If middle managers have superiors who offer them support, resources, and realism, and who trust them enough to do their jobs without micromanaging them, then they are much less likely to experience health and performance issues—and much more likely to help their organizations succeed.

In this book we will explain what the purpose of a middle manager actually is, and what the best ones actually do. We will show how management trends over the last several decades have led to a serious disconnect between the perception and actual value of middle managers. We will argue that rather than promoting the best middle managers *out* of the role, they can be promoted *within* it.

The time is right to focus on managers because the nature of work is changing at a breakneck pace, requiring a new set of people skills. Workplace communication, while easier than ever because of advanced technology, is also more abundant, complex, and confusing than ever. Automation is altering which tasks can be done by humans and which by machines, making some people's jobs obsolete. And the rise of remote work, accelerated by the pandemic, has led to a fraying of the ties that bind employees together.

Middle managers will play a vital role in dealing with all of these shifts, and many others. They will serve as filters and translators between the executive suite and the front line. They will rethink and rebundle jobs as they shift large swaths of workers to new roles. And they will be key to restoring the human connections that technology and the pandemic tore apart.

Over and over, as we've consulted with organizations, we have seen middle managers being overlooked as a way to improve productivity, boost retention, motivate staff, and create a shared sense of purpose. That's why we believe that their reputations, reward systems, and job roles need a serious overhaul.

We want more senior leaders to realize that if their middle managers seem unnecessary or underutilized, it's probably because they aren't being given the tools, the training, and the autonomy to do their jobs effectively.

Manager as Scapegoat

For years, middle managers have been mocked, neglected, and eliminated. They are frequently lampooned in movies and TV shows for holding futile meetings, sending useless emails, and preparing pointless reports. When an employee has a brilliant new idea, it's common to blame the middle manager for sending it to bureaucratic purgatory.

In fact, whenever something goes wrong at a company, it's easy to blame middle management, either as an individual entity or as an abstract idea. And yes, as management consultants, we know there are a fair number of ineffective and downright incompetent middle managers out there. But if you know of any who fit the negative stereotype, it's probably because they never should have been promoted into that position in the first place, or they never received the training and coaching they needed to succeed.

With the right training and practice, middle managers are in the best position to evaluate employee performance and provide feedback that's continuous rather than just a pro forma yearly review meant to create a paper trail. Once the bureaucratic shackles are removed from their duties, they are the ones who can truly understand how to get the best out of their workers. Once they are given the power to challenge outdated ways of operating, they have the ability to truly transform the workplace.

This is in stark contrast to a view that started to take hold in the 1980s: that the middle layers of management were a prime place to cut costs. Companies often put shareholder value front and center as a priority, supported by consultancies including McKinsey. And what's a great way to boost a company's stock price? By slashing payroll costs—by far the biggest expense for most employers.

Experts often advocated culling from the middle as a way to wring out the most cost savings with the least organizational damage, and thereby keep shareholders happy. And in many cases this strategy worked because some of these positions *were* redundant.

But, as is often the case with management strategy, the pendulum swung too far in the direction of shareholder value. This is clear from the authors' work with clients, where a too-thin layer was stretched and exhausted. Bill has seen this firsthand, having been part of client projects that were largely focused on company turnarounds or cutting costs, where layoffs were a quantifiable way to achieve cost savings. The simple laws of capitalism demand that costs can't outweigh revenue for long. At the same time, Bill saw that organizations that removed too many middle managers from their ranks ran the risk of realizing some dire effects on the entire organization: on performance, on productivity, and on long-term success.

When cost cutting becomes necessary, managers are the ones who can help companies carry it out in a more sustainable way. Too often we have seen a revolving door of indiscriminate layoffs after a bust and then rehires after an ensuing boom. If only senior leaders would enlist their managers to redeploy workers rather than letting them go, they would avoid a lot of disruption and lost productivity. This is hard to pull off, though, when the managers themselves are getting the axe, too.

Cutting middle managers, and then ignoring and neglecting the ones who remain, has a dire effect on turnover. If companies don't change the way they reward and promote their best middle managers, they will lose them, and in a cascading effect they'll also lose the people who worked for those managers. And thanks to websites like Glassdoor that survey what it's like to work at a company, they'll lose job applicants to companies with low scores on quality of management.

Why People Leave—and Why They Stay

The saying is true: People leave managers, not companies. That applies all the way from the front line to the C-suite. Around half of all workers have left a previous job because of a poor manager, according to a Gallup survey.[6] And according to a recent McKinsey survey, 52 percent of people who left a previous job said they did not feel valued by their managers.[7] (Fifty-four percent said they did not feel valued by their organization, and 51 percent said they did not feel a sense of belonging.)

The reverse, of course, is also true: People stay with, and are loyal to, their managers. "Quality of manager" is extremely important to job seekers of all ages, and especially to millennials, according to Gallup.

Larry is the kind of manager who causes people to stay. The executives at his former company found that out the hard way.

Larry says the senior leaders at his former employer, a transportation company, viewed everything in terms of spreadsheets. "I call them Excel managers," he said. "Everything is data to them. People are just a by-product." Even if they originally came from the front line, "They get this disconnect, and they start to live within this bubble."

He saw this play out in a disastrous way in his department of one-hundred-plus technicians. The company offered a twenty-four-hour repair service, but getting technicians to work an extra overnight shift or two was tough. So the company started offering $50 an hour extra as incentive pay for that time.

One day, Larry was called to a meeting at corporate headquarters. There were some new executives at the company who wanted to reduce costs, and they knew just how to do it: by dropping the overnight incentive pay. "They dreamed up this brilliant idea based on Excel sheets and P&Ls, and all the numbers worked out to them," Larry recalled. The PowerPoint presentation they showed Larry and the other managers was a thing of beauty.

Larry listened to the executives' spiel, and he wasn't having it. "I had a nickname in this company. They called me Maverick, and I hated that name because I'm a team player. A maverick implies he's only out for himself. But I'm always about my team."

Larry looked around the room and saw that most of his fellow middle managers were nodding their heads in agreement like bobble-heads. He knew he had to speak up.

"So I told them, 'That was a great presentation. Those Excel numbers looks really great. But how are you going to deliver this news to your staff? You expect us to go out there and explain to them how they're going to lose hundreds of dollars a shift? For coming in at three in the morning, which is a huge sacrifice?'"

Corporate was not swayed by Larry's argument, and the incentive pay was duly cut. As a result, the number of technicians who agreed to do after-hours work plummeted. Soon afterward, new Excel spreadsheets came in showing that after-hours calls were way down.

Several weeks later, Larry and the other managers were summoned to another meeting at headquarters. An executive said, "Our call rate is way down, and we need to do something about It. We've been kicking this around, and we think we should bring back the $50 an hour incentive pay." It was as though it was their brilliant idea.

There was plenty Maverick could have said at point, but he bit his tongue. All he said was, "That's a great idea."

Before Larry quit his last job in frustration, he had the lowest turnover of all the departments in the company. After he left, though, many of the people who had worked for him quit, too. And they could, because their skills were in demand.

Larry got fed up with his former company when the C-suite used the pandemic as an excuse to cut technician training—something Larry had championed. The move didn't make sense to him because the transportation industry was thriving as a result of Covid-19, and sales were way up. He felt executives were focused on reaching short-term cost-cutting targets over a long-term investment in workers.

A Shift in the Balance of Power

We have seen executives in an array of industries look myopically at their numbers and reduce head count and slash training budgets to achieve short-term gains. Excel sheets in the following quarters look great because payroll is such a huge cost. But as Larry's old company discovered, losing your best managers, along with the employees who were loyal to them, eventually exacts an even greater cost. That reality is reshaping our workforce and the way that leaders perceive their power.

Part of the issue is generational, Larry said. There are certainly exceptions, but many Gen Xers and baby boomers think sharing power will lead to chaos. Millennials and Gen Z tend not to think the same way, he said. They expect to have more autonomy and flexibility, and if they don't work for a company that gives them that, they will move to one that does, provided their skills are in demand.

A recent McKinsey survey found that flexibility was the number one reason that Gen Z workers were planning to stay in their current jobs, rating higher than receiving adequate compensation. For millennials (25–34) it was the second-most-important reason, with compensation ranking the highest.[8]

"You're not going to keep these people if you don't share your power with them," Larry said. More employees, and younger employees in particular, also want work that is energizing and meaningful, he noted.

He sees his middle management role as "making sure that people have every tool they need to accomplish their job, and to make sure

FIGURE 1-3

Labor force unemployment rate 1990–2022

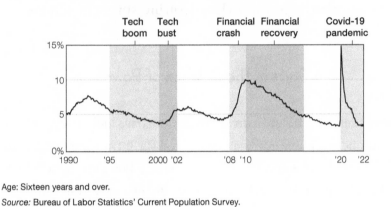

Age: Sixteen years and over.
Source: Bureau of Labor Statistics' Current Population Survey.

they have a great experience doing it. It's not just that they *can* do it, but that they love doing it."

These days, "I need to sell a vision, a value, a purpose," he said.

In survey after survey, employees have told us that they crave a sense of purpose and meaningful connections at work. Employees also want to feel valued by their managers. This was starting to happen before the pandemic, but afterward it accelerated to warp speed.

As part of the so-called Great Resignation, which was spurred by the pandemic, more people decided to drop out of the job market altogether because they felt their work wasn't giving them enough meaning and purpose. Labor force participation dropped to 62.1 percent in July 2022, compared with a sixty-plus-year peak of 67.6 percent in February of 2000 (figure 1-3).[9]

And yet many companies still assume that the only way to lure and retain workers is to increase pay and benefits. Yes, those things are helpful, but also important to many workers is that they have meaningful experiences at work. (In a 2022 McKinsey survey, we found that the prospect of doing meaningful work was the second-most-important reason why people recently took a job.[10]) And middle managers like Larry are in the best position to provide that.

By valuing and rewarding their managers, employers can turn the Great Attrition into what McKinsey has termed the Great Attraction, both retaining their best workers and enticing new ones to join them.[11]

Worthy of Reward and Recognition

What middle managers do is actually much more complex than what either executives or frontline workers do: They manage both up and down, and serve as translators in both directions. What kind of qualities and skills does the job require? Emotional intelligence, resilience, adaptability, technical skills, critical thinking, communication skills, being open to change, seeing the big picture, and managing both full-time and contract/gig workers. Everything they do deeply affects the work, the workforce, and the workplace.

For those who remained in the workforce, the pandemic made the above abundantly clear. At first, some senior leaders thought they could make all the big decisions on how things should run, but they were wrong. They came to realize that they needed middle managers more than ever. The people in the middle were the only ones who could connect the big goals at the top with the details at the bottom, and do so quickly.

And yet many of the middle managers we talked to felt they received little recognition for their accomplishments. Some felt they had no choice but to take a different job path so they could receive higher pay, bonuses, and equity.

Take Cora, who until recently was a middle manager at a pharmaceutical company with hundreds of millions in revenue. She took over a department where business had declined 10 percent and proceeded to triple its revenue in short order.

She worked eighty-hour weeks, which placed serious strain on her family life. She traveled so much (before the pandemic) that she qualified for the hard-to-get American Express Centurion card. One day she could be in Switzerland, the next in Singapore.

Considering how much she was contributing to the company and how hard she was working, Cora felt that she received far too little recognition, both in terms of appreciation and compensation. Recent research by McKinsey shows that she is not alone. Professionals in the life sciences industries said that their top reasons for planning to leave their jobs were (1) lack of career development and advancement potential (47 percent), (2) inadequate total compensation (43 percent), and (3) uncaring and uninspiring leaders (31 percent).[12]

What the best managers make is not comparable to what they contribute, she believes. "The more you get away from those middle management roles, the less relevant you become."

Cora thrived in her job. She loved being close to the action every day and making a tangible difference in her employees' lives. But she became frustrated that "the only way you can get decent equity is if you move into a C-suite." Given that that's how the system works, Cora decided to take a VP job at a medical startup that came with a large chunk of equity.

Cora and Gavin have plenty in common with many of the respondents to our survey, who also said that they did not feel sufficiently rewarded and appreciated for their work as managers.

New Job, New Outlook

Certainly Renee, the overworked manager at the clothing store, did not feel that Jane, her boss, appreciated her. Sure, one could argue that

Renee's performance was far from ideal and not worthy of praise. Jane might point to the fact that Renee's store received negative online reviews and that the pop-up she was supposed to manage did poorly.

But from Renee's point of view, she had been set up to perform poorly because the leaders above her had failed to see her potential and made her a low priority, while also giving her an impossibly wide and grueling range of tasks to perform. And that's why she handed in her resignation.

The retail industry in general clearly takes a toll on its managers. According to McKinsey research, the top reasons that retail managers left their jobs were lack of workplace flexibility (37 percent); lack of career development and advancement potential (32 percent); and poor health and well-being (27 percent).[13]

Now Renee works as a merchandising manager at a beauty company, and the difference between her old job and the new one is like night and day. Renee's new boss, Anita, checks in with her daily on Slack, over Zoom, and frequently in person.

"Really being physically present says so much more than a phone call," Renee says. "It's so much more validating than someone on the phone looking at a piece of paper and talking about metrics."

Anita collaborates with Renee rather than giving her orders. She makes sure to ask Renee how she's feeling, both on a personal and professional level, and to get a sense of whether there are any problems that she needs to help Renee solve. She makes sure Renee has the time and resources to recruit new workers, and to coach and nurture her reports.

Renee had to work on a pop-up store for this job, too. But this time was completely different. It's not that there weren't challenges. But when logistical issues threatened to delay product shipments, as an example, Anita worked with Renee to come up with a solution.

The pop-up was at a seasonal tourist spot where hiring was a real challenge. Anita trusted Renee to come up with new ways of recruiting applicants, such as using Instagram and joining a local community Facebook group. Renee also had the autonomy to interview and assess nontraditional candidates, like a hotel maintenance worker who turned out to be an excellent salesperson.

In contrast to the pop-up at her previous company, Renee was able to devote time and resources to training the staff in advance so they were familiar with the products, and to making sure that the store received attractive signage and appropriate marketing.

The beauty company does a good job of putting employees first—including managers—"which is really refreshing, because we want to feel balanced and like we're being supported, not just in our jobs but in our lives," Renee says. She can sense that flowing through to the people who work for her, too.

Renee says she hasn't cried once while on the job at this company. And that scar from her old job is fading a little each day.

TAKEAWAYS

Rethinking the Role of the Middle

The challenge: Middle managers are frustrated and exhausted from having to spend their time on activities that don't provide the most value. Instead of being free to coach and develop their team members, they report being mired in bureaucratic and individual contributor work.

How organizations can meet the challenge: Senior leaders can make a commitment to trust and empower their managers. They can strive to remove the administrative and frontline tasks that their managers currently perform so their focus is squarely on people management.

CHAPTER 2

A Look at the Forces That Got Us Here

A Technology Boom, a Financial Crash, and Then Covid-19

How, exactly, did we get to the point where middle managers have become so misused, misunderstood, and neglected? A combination of economic and societal forces led us to this point; a clearer awareness of these forces can steer us toward a more future-forward way of managing people.

Whole books have been written about the history of management. We only have room to give you the Cliffs Notes version here. What we want to make especially clear is that in the last twenty-five years, three major events resulted in a profound misunderstanding of managers' purpose: the technology boom of the 1990s and early 2000s, the financial crisis of 2008, and the pandemic of 2020.

After each of these convulsions, many senior leaders failed to see that their middle managers' roles needed to be reimagined. Instead, the C-suite allowed managers to muddle along in outmoded ways.

Either that, or the middle management layer developed late and haphazardly. Or whole layers of managers were eliminated in the name of efficiency and cost savings.

It wasn't always that way. As far back as the Industrial Revolution, organizations relied on managers in the middle to communicate up and down, assign tasks, and measure productivity. Into the 1950s and beyond, companies of any scale and complexity continued to operate as fairly rigid hierarchies, and the layers of people between the front line and the executive suite were central to execution.

It was typical for people to start at the bottom of one of these large companies and slowly work their way up to middle management. Because they often stayed at the same company for long stretches, if not their entire career, it was worthwhile for companies to invest extensively in training and rewarding them.

William Whyte described the ascent of the "Organization Man" in his book by the same name, arguing that this model contributed to stultifying conformity as workers sacrificed their individuality to the overarching goals of their organization.[1] But the hierarchical model also had real benefits, with middle managers providing stability, expertise, and institutional knowledge. Research shows that productivity grew from 1900 to 1980 as the overall share of middle management jobs increased at U.S. organizations.[2]

From the 1950s and into the '80s, the middle manager was critical as a linchpin between the upper and lower levels of the hierarchy, notes Jeff Cava, a former human resource executive at companies including Nike and Starwood who started his career in the 1970s. Without the workplace technology of later decades, only middle managers held vital pieces of knowledge. And as we all know, knowledge is power.

"Managing by walking around was a term we used a lot in the 70s and 80s," says Cava. "I'm not a particularly warm and fuzzy individual, but I still found that being able to have a meaningful conversation with superiors and subordinates throughout my career was probably one of the most important ways for me both to get things done and to learn."

It wasn't just that the middle managers held the information. They also knew how to filter and disseminate it. And for this they were highly prized.

Losing Their Status

All of that started to change in the 1990s. The rise of revolutionary new technology began to co-opt the middle manager's communication role. No longer did a CEO need to instruct a middle manager to send an interoffice memo to seventeen people separately. Instead, the CEO could choose to skip the middle manager entirely and send a single email to all seventeen people at once. No longer did a company need a middle manager to measure productivity or prepare budgets; a computer program could do that.

A 1992 article in the *McKinsey Quarterly* hailed a new management era, noting that "the basic bureaucratic organizational approach that has dominated industrial companies since the 1910s is out of date with today's needs."[3] The organizations of the 1990s must be more team-based than hierarchical, with structures that are more likely to be flat, flexible, and self-managed, the author asserted.

Advances in automation and communications technology reduced transaction costs between firms and departments. The advances allowed more jobs to be moved offshore and for more functions to be centralized. Companies could keep growing because they saved costs through employing workers in places like China, India, and Mexico. That left fewer workers to manage in the home office. And with more computers performing more work, companies' need to hire skilled technology workers became urgent, with the demand far exceeding the supply.

The conventional wisdom began to spread that middle managers might actually be unnecessary, and in fact were a drag on both efficiency and creativity. In some corners they were perceived as little more than an obstacle to relaying the insights and energies of the front line onward to senior leadership.

The 1993 book *Re-engineering the Corporation*, by Michael Hammer and James Champy, urged a radically streamlined approach to running a business.[4] For many executives, it seemed like a win-win situation: By eliminating middle managers they could both increase productivity *and* cut costs.

Into this environment, as a kind of shot across the bow, came an article titled "The War for Talent" published in the late 1990s in the *McKinsey Quarterly* and later to become a book published by Harvard Business School Press.[5] In it, the authors argued that senior leaders needed to focus on attracting the best and the brightest, the very most elite and highly skilled workers, in order to survive and thrive.

The message in "The War for Talent" was astute and well timed, but it had an unfortunate side effect: By zeroing in on elite knowledge workers, it seemed to imply that other workers were lesser or even expendable. That mentality tended to further de-emphasize the importance of middle management.

The internet bubble may have burst in 2000, but the technologies that it spawned furthered the push toward flatter organizations. Middle managers who stayed in place tended not to be valued for their proactive engagement and inspiration of the front line. Instead, some managers started to take on the role of "umbrella protectors," seeing it as their role to shield their reports from the unreasonable demands of senior leaders.[6]

The location strategy of organizations in the late 1990s and early 2000s still centered on the time-honored tradition of gathering workers together at a large physical headquarters, generally in a key metropolitan area. Many larger companies also placed hubs in important smaller markets where production and labor costs were lower.

Even as the dot-coms spread technology that enabled far-flung communication, they still adhered to the model of bringing people to the work rather than the work to the people. In this way, employees with effective middle managers could still gain the benefits of "management by walking around."

The Crash Accelerates Everything

Then came the global financial crisis of 2008. Unlike in 2000, all companies felt the effects of the crash, and some found themselves in crisis mode. The question became: Now that we're seriously strapped for cash, how do we keep the lights on? Leaders realized that they needed to significantly restructure their operations. In some cases leaders determined the answer was to eliminate people.

Over 8.8 million jobs were lost in the United States during the global financial crisis, accounting for one in five workers.[7] This meant organizations ended up with even smaller in-office workforces. Employers also sought to reduce their physical office space in order to preserve their already strained financial resources.

Management consulting companies including McKinsey were a participant in this as they worked to find ways for companies to survive the Great Recession by leveraging new technologies and new ways of working. An obvious target for cuts was the middle management layer. The senior leaders who made the decisions weren't going to fire themselves, after all. And the people at the bottom were doing the actual work. On the other hand, middle managers were getting big paychecks but didn't seem to be adding much value.

The Great Recession served to "complete the play," so to speak, in terms of finding efficiencies at the managerial level, bringing to fruition the trends that began in the 1990s. While traditional managers did take a big hit at the beginning of the recession, managerial roles grew overall as the economy recovered. But in the new knowledge economy, the nature of a manager's work often changed.

By now, organizations were confidently expanding into the virtual realm, to the point that they could interact with both employees and customers anywhere in the world. It became possible to hire both permanent and contract workers in far-flung locations. Advances in online technology meant that providing product information to customers, and processing their orders and payments, could now be reliably conducted online.

Meanwhile, growing pains emerged in many of the new, smaller offices. Many companies ditched private offices and separate cubicles altogether in favor of more open workstations. In some companies where people both worked from home and came into the office, employees did not even have their own desks, but rather migrated to whichever workstations were available that day.

It was thought that moving people closer together would foster greater collaboration and collegiality. In fact, the opposite often turned out to be true. Studies found that working in closer proximity with other workers actually increased distractions and lowered concentration, hurting productivity.[8] Managers were crucial to adapting to these new working models, and slow progress started to occur.

In the 2010s the dramatic growth of big tech gave rise to new complexities that included remote work, the gig economy, and the effects of startup competition. This brought new and shifting dimensions to the manager's mission.

Pivoting after the Pandemic

And then came the pandemic. Much in the way that the Great Recession accelerated preexisting trends, so did Covid-19—this time at warp speed. Almost overnight, organizations had to shift significant portions of their operations to remote work and rethink how and where work could be done. It was a huge challenge to come up with solutions that served employers, workers, and customers.

Operating in an emergency mode in which the rules and accepted wisdom were constantly changing proved to be a severe strain, and it exacted a huge toll on employees' mental health, middle managers included. Employers and their managers had to contend with the blurring of work-life boundaries. Some employees reveled in the flexibility that working from home offered. But others felt as if they had to be "always on" for their employers, leading to burnout. Workers also had to cope with sudden isolation from coworkers and friends, and the challenge of being both a parent and a worker when children had to be homeschooled.

After the initial intensity of the live experiment in remote work, organizations began to take stock. It became clear that more work could be done remotely than anyone had thought possible. But it was also clear that an exclusively remote working model, although possible for some job types, might not be ideal in terms of collaboration, strengthening employee connections, and solidifying company culture. After concluding that working only from home was sometimes, but not always, conducive to productivity and mental health, organizations began to envision a post-pandemic hybrid work model.

But it has taken too long for many leaders to realize that the pandemic has ushered in a new era of work—one in which middle managers need time, training, and encouragement to craft unique, department-specific solutions to workplace challenges that have never existed before.

Summing Up the Five Main Trends

We have identified five main ways in which the sweeping trends of the last twenty-five years have stunted the growth and potential of middle managers. Our hope is that recognizing them can help organizations wipe out misguided and obsolete beliefs on a path toward transforming the way people are managed.

1. Productivity advances led to "make work" and added bureaucracy

With the invention of technologies like the personal computer, the internet, and email, middle managers' roles became less critical. Realizing that their jobs were under threat, managers started to "make work" for themselves to justify their existence (or just to fill time or alleviate boredom), leading to a phenomenon known as administrivia.

This quickly became annoying and frustrating to other employees. Was it really necessary to have yet another meeting or respond to yet another email about a new project? Wouldn't it be more productive to just *work* on the new project? Middle managers were filling their time by wasting other people's time. It seemed as if their main job was just to nag everyone.

The stereotype of the middle manager as a box-checking bureaucrat reached its satirical apotheosis in the 1999 film *Office Space*, in which a self-important middle manager repeatedly scolds his subordinates for failing to file their TPS reports (purpose unknown) with a cover sheet.[9]

We're familiar with a company that got caught in the make-work trap. It decided to form a new administrative structure that was meant to combine a broad range of the company's capabilities into targeted offerings for its customers. But this well-intentioned effort turned into an administrative hell: Meetings started to multiply. It became very hard for anyone to take charge because funding models were opaque and required multiple rounds of discussions. Various micro-cells formed within the initiative, and communication between these cells was difficult. More and more staff were required to manage the complexity that had arisen, with more people adding more forms to fill out (the company's own version of TPS reports).

To stop the madness, the company put a freeze on all growth in that area, which was a very blunt instrument that did not get at the root causes of the problem—and just created more work. Eventually, the company realized that all this administrivia reflected the unit's growing pains, and it finally came up with ways of managing people that allowed for clearer communication, and fewer meetings and forms.

Senior leaders also got into a bad habit of using their middle managers to paper over bad business practices. Say an executive was having a hard time finding engineers. He might hand the assignment to a middle manager, who would experience the same trouble. The middle manager would then be blamed for failing to complete the assignment when the real problem might stem from a flawed recruiting process (not crafting the job criteria well, not working with the right recruiting sources, etc.) that needed to be revamped.

A gradual loss of autonomy, fear for their jobs, and a box-checking mentality has led too middle managers to serve as unthinking underlings. Rather than feeling empowered to question their superiors or generate their own ideas, they have come to see their role as extenders and enforcers of the status quo.

2. The war for talent created superstars and "dim lights"

Further tech progress (e.g., increased processing power, the rise of search engines and e-commerce) drove more demand for knowledge work and specialized skills. As prescribed in "The War for Talent," there was a push for companies to attract superstars. The superstar approach was so accepted that it moved far beyond the tech industry. The flip side of this was that most workers did not qualify as superstars.

In particular, companies started to turn a critical eye toward the middle managers who were not stars, and, as noted, seemed to exist for the purpose of making work. Senior leaders asked themselves: Why do I need to deal with this person in the middle who's just annoying me all the time? These perceived "dim lights" were not just people to be tolerated but actively needed to be eliminated (or de-layered) to stop an incessant flow of low-value work.

The financial crisis of 2008 put middle managers under further threat as organizations needed to cut costs, and they cut deep at the middle manager level. This gave way to the rise of more player-coach models of management, where the middle manager was no longer just part of the "meeting class" but also had to produce. This had the advantage of keeping middle managers closer to the work but also limited their ability to coach and develop others.

After the first throes of the financial crisis abated, sometimes the laid-off middle managers returned—not as full-time employees but as contractors. But the contractors were not empowered to lead other people because no one reported to them anymore. So they solely performed their former "player" role, and whole groups of employees no longer received guidance on how to grow and improve.

It soon became clear that not only do you need superstars but you also need someone to manage them and their teams. A common strategy was to promote the superstars themselves into management roles. Sometimes this worked out, but all too often it didn't, because not all individual contributors are meant to be people managers.

Laurence J. Peter came up with the Peter Principle—the notion that employees are promoted to their level of incompetence—in the 1960s. But this tendency went into overdrive in the 1990s and 2000s. We saw it happen at a law firm where all partners were expected to play a meaningful people leadership role. The firm hired a combination of Ivy League graduates and state school grads, and the latter ran circles around the former in terms of people skills.

There was a reason the Harvard grads hadn't gotten jobs at a top-tier firm: They tended to be brilliant but also eccentric. Because of the superstar mentality, some very awkward people were promoted into people management, and the firm developed a reputation as a terrible place to work—even though the lawyers there worked an average of 20 percent fewer hours than those at top-ten firms. The lawyers might have spent less time working, but their experience at work was terrible.

The firm's leaders eventually saw the light: to attract great talent, their associates had to have a great experience, and for the associates to have a great experience, their middle managers had to be outstanding.

Some of the eccentric Ivy Leaguers could be "de-weirded," so to speak, through management training and being taught how to develop their teams. But in other cases, the firm realized that it would be better to have some of the partners solely perform the roles in which they truly excelled, such as serving as rainmakers or tacticians, and still reward them handsomely.

We've also seen the superstar phenomenon play out in pharma and biotech. Take, for example, someone who is an outstanding researcher and sees patterns in the data that make them gifted at generating scientific insights. Based on their excellence as an individual contributor, they are promoted into a people leadership role. But often, these people are not natural leaders, and they can become frustrated that others on their team aren't as brilliant and insightful as they are. They ignore, berate, and sometimes even scream at their reports, resulting in widespread alienation and burnout among the non-superstars, who could still make major contributions if only they were nurtured and treated respectfully.

Fortunately, more firms are recognizing that many individual contributors can just keep doing what they're doing. Some have created promotion and compensation paths that reward superstars. The superstars are celebrated without being required to take on management roles that would just dilute their strengths.

Still, the idea that technical superstars *must* be promoted into management persists at many companies. There is no assessment to determine whether this person will excel in the new role. We know of one technical genius who was forced to leave a transportation company because he was given a choice: Either stay where you are analyzing data and make the same amount of money with the same title, or move onto a management track and make a lot more money. This man had worked for ten years in network and schedule planning for the company. Considering a merger? He could outline the revenue implication at a route level. Rationalizing a network to optimize for cost? He could find the sweet spot between operational efficiency and maximizing revenue. However, this man didn't want to be a people leader, and the company didn't want to promote him otherwise. So, after ten years of excellent work, but no career progression, he felt he had no choice but to leave.

He finished his career at a different company that knew how to recognize and reward an individual contributor—a gain for that company and a loss for his former employer, which reflexively linked career progression to becoming a manager.

3. Permafrost started to form in the middle

In some organizations where low market pressure exists (for example, at utilities and government agencies, and at legacy companies like the one we described in the previous anecdote), career middle management settled into a permafrost layer. In contrast to companies that always had a keen eye on the market—and that were constantly looking to gain an edge in talent, cost, and efficiency—these organizations largely left the middle alone over time.

Senior leaders neither cut these managers nor developed or redeployed them as true people leaders. The managers weren't totally useless: Because of their long tenure, they did have institutional knowledge to contribute. But mostly they were just left to freeze in place, with all their "make-work" meetings and processes slowing the metabolism of their organizations.

Crushing Their Spirits

The story of an East Coast technology company shows how the effects of permafrost can stifle an organization without senior leaders even being aware of it.

For a long while, the company had been considered something of a lumbering dinosaur in the semiconductor and sensor industry where it had operated for decades, after starting out as a machine parts company in the early twentieth century. Slowly but surely, decades of dysfunctional bureaucracy had caked and hardened at this company's middle layer.

But now the company had come up with a truly revolutionary environmental application for its sensors, something that promised to be a real game changer that would give some of its startup competitors a run for their money. Executives were genuinely excited about the new technology. They loved talking about the potential it had to save lives and to help fight climate change. They noted that even though the technology was brand new, it still aligned with the parts company's original mission in 1920 to "help the world run more safely and efficiently." That made for a perfect, and authentic, motivational story for the leaders to tell.

When the chief executive gave a companywide speech about the technology, the company's frontline workers were transfixed and went back to their desks feeling truly inspired. Some had friends who had ribbed them about working for such an uncool company. Now they felt validated by their decision to join the company, which was about to vault to the cutting edge.

But there was one group of employees who crossed their arms and sat stone-faced during the CEO's speech: middle managers. They did not seem enthusiastic about the new technology. This was confirmed when the company performed an organizational health survey. The middle managers had by far the lowest scores of any group of employees, both when it came to their opinion of the project and the company as a whole. They were a black hole of cynicism and resistance to change.

In-depth interviews with the managers—most of whom had been at the company for more than ten years—helped reveal why this had happened: They had been through this many times before. The first and maybe the second time they had fallen for it. But they weren't going to look like fools this time.

How were they to know that this time really was different? They had experienced several changes in leadership during which executives had given similar speeches about changing the world. But when these middle managers had jumped in and willingly given up nights, weekends, and vacations to make the new initiative a reality, or when they had tried to be creative and innovative, something always went wrong.

One manager, realizing that two departments that normally never interacted would need to start collaborating, arranged for the two groups to attend a baseball game together. Later she had her hands slapped for misusing the company expense account. Another kept working on a promising new effort without being told that it had quietly been canceled months earlier. Still another had been overwhelmed by a blizzard of forms and permissions that the company seemed to think a new project required.

All of these experiences added up for the middle managers until their spirits were crushed and they were drained of any purpose they originally had. And we can't really blame them for feeling that way.

Leaders at the technology company had to work hard to chip away at the permafrost. They had to uncover the hidden mindsets that caused the managers to resist anything new. They had to remove any real or perceived obstacles that the managers understandably foresaw. And they had to communicate and collaborate with their managers on a regular basis to make sure the project moved forward.

One manager was pleasantly surprised when he saw that the project was showing real signs of progress. He started out as a skeptic and turned into a believer. Eight months in, he told his own boss, "I thought this was going to be over four months ago."

We've worked with companies that develop regular cycles of permafrost over a period of five to eight years. Because of poor organizational design, they start moving too many managers into the middle. This results in VPs reporting to VPs reporting to VPs, with very little substantive work coming out of it.

Sometimes, a permafrost manager's greatest skill is knowing how to survive. They use the machinery of the middle to slow things down and de-motivate the people below them. These organizational fossils help give all middle managers a bad name.

The permafrost can start to melt when cost pressures emerge, and executives have no choice but to reduce head count. Guess who's the most expensive and expendable type of worker? It's the middle manager who's turned into a fossil underneath the permafrost.

But as we noted in the example of the legacy technology company, the permafrost sometimes develops for a very good reason: when middle managers become so jaded by past experience that they don't believe real change can happen at their organizations. If senior leaders take responsibility for that, they will go a long way toward challenging the hidden assumptions that prevent their middle managers from moving forward.

4. Hypergrowth led to a toxic layer of middle management, or no layer at all

In the 2000s and 2010s, we saw the rise of hypergrowth firms. They started from small bases and used their platforms or new technologies to scale rapidly. These companies included everyone from Uber to Facebook to WeWork to Netflix to HR tech unicorns, to fast-growing biotech firms leveraging new breakthroughs.

At first, some of these "flatter faster" organizations thought they didn't need middle managers and could operate with self-forming teams. But as these companies rapidly scaled, they needed to transition from a small startup culture of leaders to a broader organization with billions of customers and revenue.

While some organizations recognized this from the outset and invested early in people leaders (Netflix comes to mind), others found themselves growing without ever knowing what good managers looked like. As a result, middle managers were not consistently taught people management, and employees' experience and internal career development suffered. In the worst cases, litigation ensued because of a toxic "bro" culture in the middle ranks that infected the entire company.

Relying on Battlefield Promotions

As the CEO of fast-growing biotech firm on the West Coast discovered several years ago, at a certain point execution just isn't possible without some kind of middle layer.

The startup had developed a drug that cured a fatal disease, and it was poised to introduce several more such drugs. The CEO, Delia, still fondly remembered the time when she and her two cofounders plus two employees shared a small lab space, working against the odds to develop a life-saving drug. Together they experienced that eureka moment when they knew they were really onto something.

Then, when clinical trials showed results that exceeded their wildest hopes, the company suddenly went into high gear, going on a hiring tear for several years as venture capital money poured in. Flush with cash, the company hired the best scientists, engineers, salespeople, and marketing experts that it could find. Now, after ten years, the company had 700 employees, a $10 billion valuation, and its own building on a biotech campus. What it didn't have was an experienced layer of middle managers.

Five years earlier, the company had barely had any managers at all, having put all its hiring muscle into frontline workers. But this soon became untenable, as turf wars, communication breakdowns, systemic failures, and a host of other problems emerged. The company's structure had become too complex to survive without the mediating hand of managers. Delia, like all CEOs of startups, was being pulled in a million different directions. So she responded to the problem in the way that saved her the most time: She made a series of battlefield promotions, plucking people from the front ranks to serve as managers.

But almost none of these newly minted managers had experience managing people. They had previously worked as biochemists or epidemiologists or software developers or marketing specialists. They were all well-meaning people, and some did a better job than others, but none of them had received management training. Delia began to hear complaints about departments not cooperating and collaborating, and about important assignments falling through the cracks. She was also hearing negative comments about performance evaluations. Too many employees felt they were being blindsided with criticism about their performance at their yearly evaluations, with their compensation and bonuses taking a hit. At the same time, too many managers couldn't understand why their reports weren't performing as well as they could be.

One of those managers, Zoe, had been thrust suddenly into a management role after working for two years as a digital marketing specialist. Zoe knew that one of her reports, Brianna, was having problems prioritizing projects, but waited until Brianna's yearly performance evaluation to bring up the issue. At first Zoe felt she was discussing the problem tactfully and respectfully, but it became clear that Brianna felt blindsided.

Upset over the interaction, Zoe talked to Delia about it. Delia knew that Zoe meant well and had the potential to be an outstanding manager. The reason that the evaluation didn't go well, Delia realized, was more her fault than Zoe's.

Having heard similar stories about other evaluations, Delia knew that it was time for her to put her managers front and center. She needed to invest in training them so they knew how to coach and develop their employees throughout the year rather than simply performing annual reviews. The result was a quantifiable improvement in employee productivity.

5. Remote work removed managers from the scene—or made their jobs untenable

Before the pandemic, remote and hybrid work—supported by technology that enabled off-site collaboration and project management—was already on the rise. The pandemic vastly accelerated this new way of working. And it led to a new trend: the remote and senior individual contributor.

Whether they were partners at a law firm or senior investors in private equity, these former team leaders found they were much more productive—and happy—when they didn't have to come into the office. And they used the pandemic as an excuse to abdicate their people responsibilities. All on their own, they decided to pull a vanishing act, and the confusion of the pandemic allowed them to do it.

We saw this happening at a New York investment firm. Managers there had worked very hard in the first years of their careers doing things like grinding out financial models. They were promoted to managing director and eventually partner and made millions a year. They fulfilled the management portion of their roles with varying degrees of success until the pandemic hit, and then they just stopped. Sitting in their home office in the Hamptons, they thought, *I've got a great house with a great view, and I can work out in the morning. I don't have to deal with the city. I can do everything from here. This is wonderful! Thank you, pandemic.*

When a deal needed to be done, or an emergency happened, these managers worked hard and were accessible. But they didn't see a need to check in on their remote employees regularly. It turned out that the employees at this and many other firms suffered from their managers' absence, sometimes deeply. The managers may have rationalized that technologies like Slack and Zoom were taking over their former roles quite well. And it's true that technology has simplified the traditional managerial tasks of communication and project management. But with the pandemic, the need for human-centered leadership, empathy, and the ability to inspire and lead teams increased exponentially.

Organizations that were purpose-driven and people-focused prevailed and thrived in the pandemic. Organizations where these elements were absent suffered huge talent losses and helped fuel the Great Resignation. Surveys revealed that "not feeling valued by my manager" and "not feeling valued by my organization" were primary reasons that employees quit their jobs.[10]

In a world where teams are highly dispersed, where more work is remote, and more decisions are decentralized, it becomes harder and harder to preserve a sense of human connection, organizational culture, and shared purpose. It's up to middle managers to fill that role.

During the pandemic, some middle managers *did* step in to solve sudden and unprecedented challenges, such as how to transition an entire office to remote work. And yet too many felt they did not receive sufficient recognition or reward for their efforts. And some managers *did* take care to acknowledge and address the severe mental strain that the pandemic placed on their employees' lives—while too often neglecting their own mental health.

A 2022 survey by Future Forum, a unit of Slack Technology, found that 43 percent of managers said they were burned out, the most of any job level.[11] And the stress shows no sign of letting up. According to a *Bloomberg* article about the survey, middle managers "are now under increasing pressure from higher-ups to deliver amid economic uncertainty and concerns about declining productivity, while at the same time hearing from their employees whose compensation is not keeping up with inflation. And from the onset of the pandemic they've been tasked with navigating the challenges of leading remote and hybrid teams."[12]

Where to From Here?

We see several important dimensions emerging for middle managers in the future. With change and disruption being a constant for most organizations, middle managers will be at the heart of organizational identity. Their ability to share a sense of purpose will allow their organizations to respond quickly to challenges no matter how chaotic things become.

Yes, we have fewer barriers to communication with new technology, but nonstop proliferation of information does not lead to understanding. Hence, the best middle managers are master explainers. They separate the real signals from the noise and help convey ideas, strategies, and assignments in simple language to build common understanding across teams and organizations.

The democratization of information has become overwhelming, says Jeff Cava. Now that it's so easy for information to cascade from the very top to the very bottom, it's essential that middle managers resurrect their former roles as explainers and translators. If you spend hours explaining a company's acquisition and divestiture strategy to the line level of employee, you very well might be wasting their time, Cava says: "Different parts of the organization need different kinds of information, and they need the same information delivered in different ways." And that's an important task.

Outstanding middle managers possess a mix of excellent operational skills and true compassion at the individual level. They promote psychological safety and empowerment of individuals, creating an environment where their people feel valued.

In some ways, we could benefit from a return to the "management by walking around" that was so successful in the 1950s—but in a manner that accommodates the complex reality of new technology and hybrid work. That is going to be an arduous task, and one for which middle managers must be developed, valued, and rewarded much more intensively than they are today.

TAKEAWAYS

Rethinking the Role of the Middle

The challenge: Economic events and technological advances over the last twenty-five years have led to five trends that have weakened the manager's role: the elevation of bureaucracy; the idolization of superstars; steadfast resistance to change in the managerial "permafrost"; chaos because of hypergrowth; and the changes that emerged amid the rise of remote work.

How organizations can meet the challenge: By reinvesting in managers and reimagining their roles, executives can undo the damaging influences of the past and transform their managers into coaches, connectors, and navigators.

PART

II

Putting Middle Managers at the Center

CHAPTER 3

The Case for Staying in the Middle

From Way Station to Destination

Do you believe any or all of the following statements? Does your boss, or your boss's boss?

> The only way someone at a company can truly advance is to be promoted out of their current role.
>
> The importance of someone's job can be measured by how many people are underneath their box on the org chart.
>
> The more senior the role, the more the person in it should be paid and rewarded.
>
> Outstanding individual contributors should be rewarded with management roles.
>
> Anyone who stays in a middle management role for a long time must not be very good.

Even if you try to consciously reject these ideas, they can be hard to push away. That's because they are woven into the very fabric of the corporate world. They are stubborn relics of an era when workplaces essentially stayed the same for years at a time, and when a hierarchical management model helped ensure productivity.

But the way we work is changing so rapidly that these outmoded assumptions are now doing serious damage. They are forcing people into roles that they aren't good at and don't enjoy. Cumulatively, they create an effect that can send an organization into a downward spiral.

In particular, the middle layer of management is suffering from these false beliefs, and for three main reasons:

1. Senior leadership feels a magnetic pull to promote top middle managers into positions where they no longer do what they love: coach and connect people.

2. Senior leaders also persist in promoting their best individual contributors, without considering their fitness for a people-leadership role.

3. Middle managers who do stay in their jobs find themselves pinioned by administrative tasks, and stymied by leaders who won't empower them to make changes.

Unfortunately, the word "middle" implies that the person in that spot is on the way to somewhere else—ideally, the top. That thinking is misguided. Instead, we need to view middle managers as being at the *center* of the action. Without their ability to connect and integrate people and tasks, an organization can cease to function effectively. That's why we think the best middle managers are best off staying exactly where they are—managers like Marcus, who refused to accept the prevailing belief systems about management.

Saying No to a Promotion

Marcus went straight into his first job without any idea of what he'd actually be doing. He only knew he wanted to "make a difference." While studying political science at a midwestern university, he was known as a defender of lost causes, which suddenly weren't so lost once he championed them. When an eighty-year-old university building—the site of some of his favorite classes—was slated for demolition, he rallied the right people so that it received a historic designation and could not be destroyed.

Marcus had big aspirations for changing society, and he thought that Washington, D.C., would be the place to achieve them. Just after graduating, he was excited to see a posting for a federal affairs coordinator at a trade group in D.C. They were looking for a "dynamic team player and a self-starter who can juggle multiple projects" while pursuing "policy and advocacy efforts on a diverse set of issues." To his delight, he got the job.

When he arrived, he was the lowest-ranking person on his team. As such, he didn't do much talking in meetings. But he was able to observe who his bosses met with, from lawmakers to lobbyists to corporate policy directors. He always noticed one group from a consumer goods company. They were animated and passionate, and it was obvious that they respected one another. Most of all, everyone on the team seemed to be having a good time.

Eventually, Marcus left for what he thought was his dream job: working as a staff member for a House committee. A few years in, though, while doing research on a consumer rights bill, he noticed that the consumer goods company he had admired in his previous job was looking to fill a government affairs position. As a defender of "the little guy," Marcus had never pictured himself working for a big corporation. But on a whim he applied. Even though his interviews had gone well, he was surprised when the hiring manager called to say that the job was his.

Marcus was a little afraid that taking the job would require him to sacrifice some of his values, but this proved not to be the case. In fact, he came to realize that he could make more changes from his corporate perch than in his past job.

In his new role, Marcus kept one foot in government while interacting with other key players across the company. In the process, his bosses discovered that he had an uncanny ability to bring people from far-flung groups together to achieve common goals. His ability to listen and work toward solutions improved how his company was perceived both inside and out.

The company enlisted Marcus's help when its plan to build a new regional office in North Carolina faced opposition from community leaders who feared it would threaten the city's small-town atmosphere. Marcus listened to their concerns and went back to his superiors and his team. The company agreed to build the office farther away from the center of town than originally planned. Also, by drawing on the experience of another regional center, Marcus devised a pilot program that would target people without college degrees who were struggling to find work in the region. Marcus's interventions helped get the company's plan unanimously approved by the city council.

When Marcus finished work for the day, he almost always felt that he had added specific and substantive value. It was a satisfying feeling. Soon he was promoted to manage his own group, and he excelled as a people leader. He demonstrated real concern for the development of his team members, and he thought carefully about how to position them for success. Alice, Marcus's boss, was thrilled to see him performing so well and didn't mind giving him credit. She sang his praises to her own bosses, so that they were well aware of this star in their midst.

Then, several years into Alice's tenure, she accepted a job as a top officer at a think tank. As she prepared to leave, Alice's bosses let

Marcus know that her vice president position was his for the asking. At first Marcus was thrilled at the opportunity. And who wouldn't be? In addition to the cachet of being a VP, he would receive a hefty salary increase, plus a large block of stock options. Despite his initial excitement, though, Marcus found himself dreading the promotion.

Alice's vice president job was important, but it didn't play to Marcus's strengths. Alice was good at planning and strategizing. She knew how to maneuver among senior leaders to get things done. When Marcus came up with a great new idea inspired by his interactions with various constituents, she was the one who could pull the right levers with senior leaders to make it happen. But she worked with a much smaller and less varied pool of people than Marcus did.

When Marcus considered what Alice actually *did* all day, the knot of anxiety in his stomach tightened. He knew that the people he wanted to interact with were the doers—his team members, the researchers, the frontline community leaders—and not just top executives. He had seen how Alice's time was squeezed by endless senior briefings.

After some soul-searching, Marcus did something that required a fair amount of fortitude: He declined to apply for Alice's job, and the company ended up hiring an external candidate as vice president. He turned down the promotion because he enjoyed the job he was doing. It was fun for Marcus to meet with a wide range of people, either individually or in groups. He realized that his daily job satisfaction was more important to him than a higher paycheck.

His bosses accepted Marcus's decision with regret, but as they saw him expand his reach and influence and take on increasingly complex projects, they realized that he had made the right choice. They understood that moving him to a vice president position would have been a mistake, both for him and the company.

Marcus's actions led his company to take a hard look at its overall promotion and compensation practices. He ended up getting a promotion after all, but without having to move up the corporate ladder. He negotiated several key elements of his new role: he would have ample time to lead his team of people, and his VP would help him manage many of the time-consuming interactions with people more senior than him.

We have seen star managers like Marcus throughout our careers. They naturally attract the attention of senior leaders who want to reward and retain stellar performers, yet the reward normally comes in the form of a new job where these managers can no longer use the very skills that got them noticed in the first place. It's a huge waste of talent to see a manager who once looked forward to coming into work now sitting in a big new office drowning in abstract and administrative work that makes them miserable.

Meanwhile, senior leaders tend to retain middle managers who are good at being bureaucrats, administrators, and political players. They aren't quite bad enough to be let go, but they also aren't good enough to promote. They become a part of the organizational "permafrost" that resists change and stays stubbornly in place.

We find it maddening that so many corporations tend to keep poorly performing managers in place while promoting successful individual contributors and managers into jobs that they find dull, distasteful, and dissatisfying. It seems so obvious: If a person is passionate about their job, then let them stay where they are.

Saying Yes to a Promotion—and Regretting It

Unlike Marcus, another excellent manager was unable to resist the pull of a promotion, even though her instincts told her to stay where she was. Her story is all too common.

Kelsey was a standout manager of a big-city K-8 education center, where tutors helped children with math, reading, and computer skills.[1] She hired and trained the full- and part-time staff; interacted with parents and children; and even pulled people off the sidewalk and gave them sales pitches. She estimates that she put in about 20,000 steps a day in that job because she was constantly in motion.

Because of its unique location, the facility served students from some of the best and also some of the worst schools in the city, and yet it all just worked. The center was open seven days a week, and once Kelsey worked twenty-three straight days. Still, she thrived on the intensity of her job. She still remembers one particularly busy day when she was rushing around with sweat stains under her arms, and a couple of pencils in her messy hair. The air was filled with the excited din of children's voices as they worked with their tutors. One of the fathers, who had initially been skeptical about sending his son to the program, turned to her and said, "You guys do something pretty magical here, don't you?" To this day, it chokes her up just thinking about it.

Then the company was bought by a larger firm. That's when the trouble began. Seeing that Kelsey was a star at an individual center, a newly installed executive urged her to apply for a job as a regional manager. She got the full-court press, fancy dinner included. So how could she say no? After all, instead of being in charge of one center, she would be overseeing eight centers. That was so much more impressive, right?

Still, an inner voice kept saying, "Don't do it." But when she expressed doubts to her friends, they said, "You'd be a fool to turn it down. You're getting a raise, and it will look great on your resume."

So she took the job—and was miserable.

A big part of her new job was checking in with the managers of the other centers, making sure they were doing their jobs properly. She also needed to ensure that they were meeting their financial targets each month, which turned out to be impossible because the centers were coming off a boom year that was unrepeatable.

The executive who promoted her had tried to seal the deal by promising that Kelsey could work from home most of the time. There was just one problem—she didn't *like* working from home. She missed the conferences, the coaching, and the constant buzz that used to surround her each day.

One day, while Kelsey was sitting alone in her apartment checking out the latest P&Ls, her boss called to ask her about the maintenance plan at one of the suburban centers. That's when she knew she couldn't take it much longer. Not much later, she quit her job and applied for a teaching fellowship program at a public school system. Now she teaches junior high English.

The sad thing, Kelsey says, is that she would have been a lifer at the for-profit education company if only top leaders had known how to nurture and reward her as a middle manager.

The Waffle House Way

With much of the corporate world still in the dark about how to promote stars within the same role, we direct attention to the promotion practices of an iconic restaurant as an example of how to do it right.[2]

If you've driven highways in the South, you most likely have stopped at a Waffle House. The beloved restaurant chain has more than 2,000 locations, primarily in states such as Florida, North Carolina, Alabama, and Georgia, where the first Waffle House opened in 1955. The chain prides itself on its doors never closing, which makes it a favorite of long-haul truckers and just about anyone with a 2 a.m. hankering for its famous waffles or hash browns served "covered," meaning topped with a slice of cheese, or "chunked," with cubes of ham added.

New grill operators at Waffle House start with the title of, well, grill operator. In addition to learning how to make each dish to the chain's exacting standards, they have to master Waffle House's shorthand for servers to signal to grill operators what to make for each plate. If a plate comes to the kitchen with a mustard packet turned up, the grill operator knows the customer wants Papa Joe's Pork Chop and Eggs; mustard packet side down means Country Ham and Eggs. If a plate comes in with a pat of butter, it's for the T-Bone and Eggs, but the location of the butter matters: top of the plate means well done, bottom means rare.

With experience and training, these employees have an opportunity to rise to the level of master grill operator. Master operators, after passing tests that demonstrate their knowledge of customer service, food safety, and cooking, not to mention Waffle House's lore and practices, then receive a higher salary and more responsibilities.

After demonstrating further mastery of techniques and safety certifications, as well as generating a consistent average of $6,000 in revenue per shift (at an average price of less than $10 per order, mind you), these grill operators receive another generous salary boost and get to call themselves the honorific of "Elvis of the Grill." While some of those who achieve this level take on additional responsibilities to train newbies, the goal is to keep them doing what they do best— because without quality grill operators, the restaurants couldn't maintain their trademark dishes or 24-7 schedule.

If Waffle House can get this concept right, why can't the rest of the corporate world?

The trades, at least, have long understood the value of promoting people within the same job. Someone who trains to be an electrician is an electrician for life, beginning as an apprentice, rising to become a journeyman, and closing their career as a master electrician, with corresponding jumps in pay and responsibilities. Smart companies have been applying this same concept to technical positions by creating technical career tracks for top performers rather than promoting them to team lead roles that would take them away from their excellent contributions.

We know of one tech executive who spent years thinking that the only way he could reward his best software engineers was to move them into people management roles. When he finally realized that this assumption was misguided, he thought it would be enough to set up separate promotional tracks for the engineers. But to his surprise, this wasn't the "build it and they will come" scenario that he had envisioned. That's because leaders hadn't made the changes management required to keep these pathways fully operational and attractive to employees. His star employees, too, needed to unlearn the idea that staying in individual contributor roles was somehow unacceptable. The company needed to build a new employee value proposition for its rock star tech talent who derived their energy from technical work rather than managing others' work.

The tech executive deeply regrets not learning this sooner, because he knows he lost some of his best talent by pushing them into management positions that were not right for them.

We believe that organizations will reap huge benefits if this concept spreads much more widely to middle management, too. We have seen it over and over in our work: The people who excel at middle management jobs are true superstars. When one department or team clearly stands out from the rest, more often than not it's because of a superstar manager. Once these superstars are identified, senior leaders need to do everything in their power to keep them in their jobs. Levers at their disposal can include:

- *Salary and bonuses.* That seems like an obvious one, but it's really not. It's engrained in corporate culture to pay officers, vice presidents, and other senior leaders more than middle managers. But why? When appropriate, pay the best middle managers even *more* than your senior leaders to show how much you value them. If you hear complaints from the executives, make up the difference in equity. And the compensation can be commensurate with the value a role creates.

- *Stock and stock options.* Speaking of equity, we've been surprised to hear how little equity most middle managers receive.

Often it's zero or a pittance. Let your hardworking managers share in the equity pot, or you might just see them leave for a startup that showers them with options when they join. Yes, those startup options need to vest and they might end up being worthless, but they send an important message: If you help our company succeed, you will be mightily rewarded for it.

- *A bigger sphere.* Expand the scope or scale of what someone manages without changing the essentials of the job. School districts sometimes do this with their principals, who are—when you think about it—the quintessential middle managers. Rather than promoting them into a superintendent role, which removes them from the teacher-student action, enlightened school districts will place them in a much bigger school instead. In the retail sector, a company might move an excellent manager from a smaller store to a superstore, or give them hiring, training, and coaching duties at several additional stores.

- *Title changes.* In the case of a store manager, a person's title might change from junior manager to senior manager to executive manager as their sphere of influence grows. But these title changes can't be no-cost empty words. A new title can come with measurable rewards and increased responsibility while still keeping the job's focus at the center of the action.

- *Challenging assignments.* Every great manager we've met always has ideas about how to make things better. Ask your best ones what they would do if they were in charge. Then, if they're willing, put them in charge of their great idea.

- *Flexible working arrangements.* Just as middle managers can make every effort to accommodate the needs and preferences of their reports, so can managers receive that same consideration from their bosses.

How can you make sure you are offering the right rewards to your most-valued managers? Here's a thought: Ask them! Some may appreciate a bump in salary; others may value more time off. Still others may want a coveted assignment or a travel opportunity. Tailor your rewards to the priorities of your managers.

The way we see it, superstar managers are like the head coach of a football team. After their team wins the Super Bowl, team owners reward and celebrate the coach with accolades, bonuses, and a fat contract renewal. What they don't do is show appreciation by saying, "Congratulations, I'm moving you to the front office." But that's exactly what many companies do.

Make It the Number One Priority

We can see some executives rolling their eyes and thinking, *But I can't afford to give my best middle managers big raises. Plus, I can't change their job description; they already have too much to do.*

We're here to say: Yes, you can make these changes. Here's how:

By now, everyone in the corporate world is aware of how automation, artificial intelligence, and machine learning threaten to disrupt every kind of enterprise from factories to retailers to white-collar professions. A recent study found that when companies adopted artificial intelligence, managerial positions—not frontline workers—took the biggest hit.[3] Executives frequently cut management jobs in a shortsighted attempt to save money. No wonder managers operate from a place of fear.

We're willing to bet that companies are failing to see the huge opportunities that arise when middle managers are free to pursue work that focuses on people rather than procedures. A thorough, honest inventory of current managerial jobs would yield abundant duties that a machine can perform: make sure employees show up on time, track how much sick time and vacation time they take, inspect their work, check various analyses and calculations, and so on. At many companies, these jobs are still done by managers due to sheer inertia and resistance to change; however, it won't be long before someone figures out that AI can do all those things, and much more accurately at that.

Now, for the tasks that remain after technology takes over, how many are really central to managing people? It can be eye-opening to do a thorough time inventory of a manager's day—and we recommend that as part of overhauling the job. In many cases, a manager's day is stuffed full of emails and meetings. But how many emails do middle managers really need to be sent or cc'd on? Couldn't many decisions and approvals be routed to someone else? And does a particular manager really need to attend that meeting on building a second office in Atlanta? As our survey showed, middle managers on average reported that they spent nearly three-quarters of their time on work that did not involve managing people (see figure 1-2).[4] Their bosses can pave the way for them to steer that percentage in a more healthy and productive direction.

Executives could choose to eliminate half of their management team *or* do something radically different with their managers. Imagine: What if middle managers focused exclusively on helping people work better? Once you take away administrative work that can be automated, moved to someone else, or taken away entirely, what you have left is a true manager of talent who can help people become better versions of themselves at work.

We are asking for nothing less than an entire mindset shift around middle management. Companies can't look at overhauling this role as one thing among many. It has to be *the* thing that's first on the list. Almost everything else can wait.

Work, Workforce, Workplace

When the role of the manager is reimagined, their imprint on the work, the workforce, and the workplace will be greater than no other.

First, the *work* itself. Just as automation is changing the jobs of middle managers, so is it transforming the jobs of the people they manage. It's the managers who are in the best position to look at all the work that needs to be done and to ask: What can technology do best? What can machines do best? After that is answered, what is left for people to do, and who are the best people to do it?

Next, the *workforce*. Managers with low attrition rates invest time and energy into recruiting new talent and developing the talent they have. Our McKinsey research on the "Great Attrition, Great Attraction" shows that a lack of career development is a key reason why knowledge workers quit their jobs, even without a new job lined up.[5]

And finally, the *workplace*. With more people working from home, and office configurations and real estate in a state of flux, *workplace* has become a fungible term. Managers are the glue that holds sometimes far-flung groups together, helping to resolve issues among and between teams. To meet the demands of their role, though, managers must be allowed to reinvent themselves as super-connectors, navigators, rule challengers, and talent managers.

Imagine if managers were able to spend most of their day doing the following:

- Helping their team members connect the work they do to the organizational purpose and to each individual's purpose, as this results in measurably better outcomes.

- Clarifying each team member's goals with a deep understanding of how their unique skills and strengths can contribute to the company's long-term goals.

- Helping each team member seek new assignments that allow them to develop skills and experience so they continue to grow and advance long-term career goals.

- Recognizing obstacles that stand in the way of accomplishing goals and taking concrete steps to remove them, so team members can do more with less struggle and frustration.

- Playing an active role in conflict resolution, not as a decider but through coaching and intervention to keep lines of communication clear, respectful, and productive.

- Providing frequent and nonjudgmental feedback to help each team member achieve their best performance.

- Strengthening ties among team members so that everyone understands common goals and feels they have a stake in the company.

- Connecting employees and helping them remain productive regardless of where they are doing their work, whether at headquarters, at home, at a coworking site, a coffee shop, or a hotel in Bangkok.

Instead of Michael Scott from *The Office,* the ideal manager of the future will look more like the TV soccer coach Ted Lasso: self-aware, thoughtful, vulnerable, optimistic, and adaptive. This isn't a new idea, yet consistent workplace modeling of these qualities is surprisingly rare. We believe that they should be the *primary* criteria for the hiring and evaluation of managers.

Getting started on these changes will be the most difficult part of the process, and it must be accompanied by rigorous training, because no single manager will have the high-level people skills required of their redefined jobs. But once you have trained managers in these roles, the results will be immense, and the best and brightest will clamor for these jobs.

TAKEAWAYS

Rethinking the Role of the Middle

The challenge: The role of people management has been seriously undervalued at organizations that have failed to keep pace with changing realities. It is not enough for senior leaders to communicate directly with the front line. Real coaching and mentoring must occur for these messages to truly resonate.

Why middle managers are key to meeting the challenge: Only middle managers, in their pivotal position between the C-suite and the front line, are capable of acting as consistent coaches, navigators, and connectors in an increasingly complex business world that includes remote and hybrid work, contract employees, and ever-changing external demands. In the new world of work, human capital is much more important than financial capital.

What senior leaders can do to meet the challenge: Executives can make transforming their middle management ranks their number one priority. They can indicate that these are highly desirable roles; place their most qualified and valued people into management positions; provide training so their managers can excel; promote and reward their best managers within the role instead of up and out into more senior roles; and give them time to actually manage.

CHAPTER 4

The Great Rebundling

From Job Eliminator to Job Re-Imaginer

Recently a woman entered a grocery store in Franconia, Virginia. Casually walking down the wide, clean aisles, she put into her cloth tote bag three just-ripe avocadoes, two Roma tomatoes, a bulb of garlic, and, after a quick squeeze, a single lime. Then she walked right out of the store. No outraged store employee chased after the woman demanding that she pay for her items. That's because she'd already completed her purchases without going anywhere near a cashier or a self-checkout machine.

The store, an Amazon Fresh grocery store, uses what's known as Just Walk Out technology. When the woman first entered the store, she took out her phone, tapped on an app, and scanned a QR code. From there, an array of technology including optical sensors tracked her movements as she strolled through the produce section. Every time she put an item in her tote bag, it also appeared in her virtual Amazon cart.

The sensors were sophisticated enough that once she realized that one avocado was too hard for the guacamole she was planning to make that evening, the technology took note when she replaced it with another one. If she had decided to ditch all her produce to buy the ready-made guacamole a few aisles away, it could have tracked that, too, taking all the previous items out of her virtual cart.

Once the woman left the store, Amazon charged her for the items in her virtual cart and emailed her a receipt. No having to dig for a credit card or cash. No waiting in line. No hitting the wrong button on a machine and having to call an employee over to fix it. In a previous era this behavior would have been considered stealing. Now it was just business as usual.

The first Amazon Fresh supermarket opened in Woodland Hills, California, in 2020, to great fanfare.[1] A year and a half later, about two dozen of the stores were operating across the country. In 2021 the company announced plans to add Just Walk Out technology to some of its Whole Foods stores, and to sell it to third-party retailers, meaning you may soon be using it when buying not only groceries but also hardware, toys, and clothing.

For slower adopters, Amazon still offers cashiers, along with scanning machines, at its stores. But the future is clear: technology is usurping the human role in the checkout process.

Or is it? Does the cashier's job really disappear completely if a customer can just walk out of the store?

Middle managers across all industries will be key to answering this question as the nature of work changes because of technology, automation, and shifting demands. The smartest companies will put managers at the center of an effort to rebundle jobs and connect them to the right people in a meaningful way.

Cashiers are a case in point (table 4-1). Through the years, their role has evolved from calculating prices manually and counting change to scanning soup cans, to looking up the four-digit code for avocados, to waiting for customers to swipe their credit cards, to intervening with fickle self-checkout machines.

TABLE 4-1

How cashiers can be redeployed by managers

JOB CATEGORY, SHARE OF TIME	TASK	FUTURE TIME SPENT ⇩ ▭ ⇧
Purchase execution, ~40%	Process sales or other transactions	——
	Calculate costs of goods or services	——
	Issue money, credit, or vouchers	—
Customer interaction, ~35%	Answer customer questions: goods and services and/or technical	—
	Greet customers, patrons, or visitors	—
	Sell products or services	—
Clerical tasks, ~15%	Maintain records of sales or other business transactions	——
	Stock products or parts	·
Potential new and emerging tasks, TBD	Monitor customer self-checkout station and triage any issues	
	Diagnose and repair mechanical issues with customer-facing technology	
	Transport online orders fulfilled in-store to customers in vehicles	
	Deliver online orders to customers in their homes	
	Offer in-store product demonstrations	
	Train new hires	

Source: McKinsey Global Institute Analysis, 2019.

While those transactional tasks are core to the cashier role, they are far from the sum of what a cashier does. Cashiers also answer customer questions, like where to find the non-dairy Ben and Jerry's, or when the jicama will be in stock again. For customers needing a little extra help, cashiers also work to flag down a courtesy clerk to take a heavy item like a case of water to the customer's car and place it in the trunk.

Cashiers also play an important role in greeting customers and exchanging pleasantries with, say, a regular's five-year-old grandson who's a budding soccer star. Research on "weak ties" has shown that seemingly superficial interactions with people who aren't family and close friends—the kind you develop with your local barista or store employee—have a profound effect on well-being. In short, some people *prefer* to have human contact while shopping.

An Outstanding Cashier

Walt was one of those grocery store cashiers who brightened people's moods. Unlike some of his colleagues who kept a close eye on the clock, he prided himself on his interactions with customers. Often it was just a quick hello, but not always. A man once sought his advice about where to ask the love of his life to marry him. Whatever people wanted to discuss, Walt was game.

Walt displayed the same energy for his other passion as the drummer for a heavy metal band. From the time he was eight, he aspired to be the next Lars Ulrich. He had played with the same group of friends since high school and they were steadily developing a following in Fairfax County, Virginia, and beyond. But divided among five bandmates, the payout from two or so gigs a week barely covered Walt's utility bills, let alone his rent.

That's why for the last five years, Walt happily showed up every day (except Wednesdays, when the band practiced) to work as a cashier at a large grocery store chain. It was a steady job and it was fairly easy for him to swap shifts when the band occasionally went on tour. Plus, he had health insurance, an important consideration for someone like him with type 1 diabetes.

Walt may not have dreamed of a long-term career in the grocery industry, but he still took his job seriously. In addition to pleasing customers with his personable manner, he was efficient at ringing up purchases and was always glad to lend a hand in dealing quickly with unexpected glitches.

The store's front-end manager, Tara, considered Walt to be a dream employee. She had never even heard of Lars Ulrich of Metallica; her musical tastes ran more toward Mariah Carey and Celine Dion. But she appreciated Walt so much that once (and only once) she went to one of his concerts, keeping earplugs in the whole time.

To show how much she valued Walt, Tara gave him regular raises and bonuses. But despite her praise, Walt couldn't help wondering if his days at the grocery store were numbered. After the widespread installation of self-checkout, he noticed customers waiting for the machines even when the cashier-staffed lines were shorter.

Walt was so worried about his job that when Tara took him aside on yet another slow day for him, he feared she was going to say that his services were no longer needed. But instead, Tara asked Walt if he would be interested in traveling to a weeklong program that would train him for a new customer service role at the store. In his new position, Walt would be responsible for a range of customer service needs, which would free him from spending most of his time behind the cash register.

Walt immediately said yes. A week later he found himself attending the training program in Raleigh with Bridget, whose stockroom role was being partially replaced by robots; and Carlos, an accounting office clerk whose job could now be done mainly by artificial intelligence. Fortunately for Walt, Bridget, and Carlos, their managers had identified them as valued employees and steered them toward roles that enabled them to meet emerging demands.

Unlike Walt, Tara did want to spend the rest of her career in the retail industry. Quite simply, she loved her job, especially the parts that involved dealing with people. Not that it wasn't hard and even exhausting sometimes. With a harried husband who also worked in retail, and two children under the age of eight, she often had a hard time balancing her work and her home life. Just as her own reports came to her with their struggles, she sometimes had to talk through the competing demands of her life with her own district manager.

Tara's district manager and those above her noted Tara's ability to train and coach her employees. The employee retention rate at her store was much higher than average, and they knew that was mostly because of Tara. Early in her tenure, her bosses enrolled her in a special training program at headquarters for the most promising managers throughout the company. Even so, Tara had recently been afraid that her own boss would tap her on the shoulder to say that *her* job was being eliminated. With automation and technology starting to supplant so much of the work her employees did, would her skills even be needed anymore?

The answer, she soon came to discover, was an emphatic yes. In fact, her bosses gave her a crucial assignment. Like so many other leaders looking to capitalize on emerging technology, the executives at headquarters had determined which tasks could now be performed by technology and which still hinged on the human touch. But they had no knowledge of the players who would be involved. It was up to Tara to fit the new pieces together and match the right employees with the right tasks. And just as important, she continually coached her workers as they adjusted to the demands of their reconfigured jobs.

From entry-level work to highly skilled technical jobs, as automation reinforces the need for high-value roles while eliminating rote tasks, a wide swath of companies will be engaged in what we call the Great Rebundling. Although often designed at headquarters, the actual details of the rebundling can only be carried out by those with an intricate understanding of what happens at ground level: middle managers.

Matching Talent to New Needs

It's the managers who will be at the front lines of millions of individual transactions, interactions, and processes happening across the country. These managers will be responsible for matching the right talent to the new roles, inspiring their employees, and providing individual training and coaching.

Organizations with foresight are deputizing middle managers like Tara to take the pieces of each job apart and put them back together again. It takes people experts to perform this task effectively.

Three main factors must be considered as jobs are rebundled:

Changes in price, quality, and expectations: This covers what customers will pay for goods or services and what they expect in return. For example, people are willing to pay extra for an Amazon Prime account, and in return they expect their order to come the next day, rather than waiting up to a week as they did in the past. On the other hand, they may pay less for a hardcover book listed in "fair" condition by a third-party seller, and wait longer for its arrival, if it only costs 99 cents.

Changes in volume: This includes the products and services that are in demand, and it waxes and wanes based on external forces. During a particularly hot summer, say, more air conditioners and fans must be available, and electricity rates will surge. During a particularly warm winter, demand for winter coats and accessories, along with the cost of heating, will fall.

Changes in standards: These relate to the policies and laws that determine what is allowed or required within a given industry. Think of all the new regulations around travel after the September 11 attacks.

Both government agencies and corporations had to pivot in response to the new requirements.

Based on these three factors, the need for performing certain tasks within a job will vary. Leaders who redeploy their workers to adapt to these shifts will be in the best position to meet their customers' needs and stay financially strong.

We saw demand change at warp speed during the pandemic. Many gyms closed, so everyone ordered dumbbells and other in-home exercise equipment. Sales of hand sanitizer went through the roof, leading to widespread shortages. Movie theaters were forced to close, and subscriptions to streaming services climbed. The whole restaurant experience changed, too: suddenly it was okay to eat in the street, or take home a $45 steak in a Styrofoam container.

Look at the travel industry. At first airplanes were barely flying at all, and then, for a while, they could only be one-third full for health reasons. Low demand kept passenger fares low, while cargo revenue remained high. Smart leaders quickly switched available passenger pilots to cargo flights. Meanwhile, on the reduced passenger flights, cleanliness and hygiene were paramount, food and drink an afterthought.

During the pandemic, the work that many employees did was vastly different from the work they had been trained to do. Instead of spending much of their time on food and drink service, flight attendants became hygiene enforcers. A few even had to figure out how to duct tape unruly passengers to their seats.

At Delta, airline leaders recognized that some employees wouldn't mind having time off, whereas others wanted to keep working.[2] A voluntary leave-of-absence program prevented mass furloughs. For those employees who still wanted to work, the airline activated a companywide talent network that swiftly aligned supply with demand in the form of temporary assignments.

The quick rebundling that leaders did—or didn't do—during Covid-19 determined whether a business or industry flourished, flailed, or failed. In all these areas, managers were the bridge that aligned employee skills with changing company needs.

Tara, Walt's manager at the grocery store, saw the pandemic change the world as she knew it, too. At first hardly anyone came into the store. Customers instead ordered items online and picked them up in their cars or had them delivered to their homes. She had to redeploy some of her cashiers and greeters to curbside, or enlist them as delivery people. When employees fell ill from Covid-19 or had to quarantine after being exposed to it, she moved employees to fill empty spots on the fly, and she often had to provide some impromptu training in the process.

When the pandemic eased, Tara was able to carry out her employer's rebundling plan with a firm grasp of her employees' strengths and weaknesses. She knew that Walt, her personable and efficient cashier, would be perfect for broader customer service roles. Another cashier, Dale, refurbished electronics as a hobby and turned out to be expert at handling issues with the self-checkout machines. They broke down often enough, and customers had enough problems using them, that working on them turned into a full-time job for Dale, and he enjoyed it.

Tara had noticed that another of her cashiers, Rhonda, possessed a gift for de-escalating conflicts. Once, when Rhonda saw a customer become angry because a new employee wouldn't accept an item he wanted to return, she quickly walked over to the two and demonstrated how to confirm the purchase without a receipt, while calming both the customer and the flustered employee. Later on, Tara knew that Rhonda would be an excellent addition to an expanded front-end customer relations department that existed to handle especially difficult and complex interactions—such as approaching a customer who was not charged for their order or helping someone whose online delivery had been botched. Because of her interactions with her staff and her ability to observe their work closely, Tara, not the higher-ups in corporate, had the information to optimize who went where and did what.

Altering Work as We Know It

In corporate headquarters across the country, leaders are reimagining their operations to take advantage of changing technology and changing customer preferences. For retailers, whether they envision a "just walk out" future like the one Amazon is piloting or choose a different customer service model will significantly alter the role of cashiers and many other employees.

Forward-looking leaders in a host of industries, from insurance to health care to air travel, have been asking three key questions as they redesign their operations. Let's drill down and see how this is playing out at grocery stores.

What can technology do? This includes advances in computing, artificial intelligence, and video recognition. The same types of underlying technology that power self-driving cars can also help grocery stores operate more efficiently. Deep learning, a form of artificial intelligence, can analyze data to build ever more sophisticated layers of information to guide future decisions on things like customer service, pricing, inventory management, and fraud detection.

Technology can allow for the tracking of customers that makes checkout machines unnecessary. It can also monitor how long someone's eyes linger over the Cadbury Creme Eggs in the Easter candy section—noting that this might be a personalized marketing opportunity, either now or next Easter.

It's important to remember that just because technology *can* do something, doesn't mean technology *should* do it. In some cases, privacy concerns make the monitoring of consumer behavior inadvisable or even illegal. But a full understanding of technological capabilities is central to shaping the future of work.

What can machines do? This refers to the sorting devices and material movers that can do physical tasks in the physical world. In retail, machines can help with a range of tasks, from helping to unload trucks to keeping the back room organized to cleaning floors. Machines will eventually take over much of the manual labor done by humans, but not all of it. Some of these tasks might be theoretically possible for machines but much more reliably (or cheaply) done by humans.

What can humans do? People are the most unpredictable, challenging, and rewarding part of the rebundling effort. Along with determining the roles of technology and machines, operations leaders will be crafting the human roles of the future. Customer service and interaction will be an increasingly important part of the human work in grocery stores and many other industries.

The economists Daron Acemoglu and Pascual Restrepo have warned against the rise of "so-so technologies" (they actually cite self-checkout machines, along with automated customer phone service, as examples), which seem like a good idea but do not actually result in productivity gains.[3] Companies can focus on introducing technology that significantly increases productivity and creates jobs elsewhere, they say.

Once store operations leaders understand the potential for both technology and machines, they must consider customer preferences and how the human component of rebundling can best serve them. In the case of in-store shopping, will customers no longer tolerate the experience of waiting in line? Or will some customers be willing to wait for a short time in exchange for a pleasant interaction with a cashier?

Which personalized services will a store want to maintain even though technology could theoretically replace them? For example, if a grocery store has a large selection of Jasper Hill Farm cheese from Vermont, with prices exceeding $20 per pound, should it maintain a staff of cheesemongers who can help distinguish between multiple types of "stinky" cheese on display? Or will customers be fine looking at a kiosk that has a written description of each cheese, with a floating "customer service teammate" (who may have started as a cashier) available to answer any questions?

Traditional cashier duties such as processing sales, calculating costs, and handling money and credit cards will drop in the future. And certain forms of customer interaction, while still important, will also be reduced. On the other hand, cashiers will be ideally positioned to handle a rising need for things such as delivering orders to customers' cars, offering in-store product demonstrations, and training new hires.

Senior leaders might choose, say, to merge the remaining customer interaction tasks with stocking and with transporting online orders to customers in their cars. But these role redesigns are not done in a vacuum. Leaders are also trying to understand—via surveys, focus groups, and interviews—what combination of tasks would be most enjoyable and meaningful for their workers. And they are working to understand the skills required for those tasks so they can provide the right training and conduct hiring assessments.

It's very encouraging that the world's largest private employer, Walmart, has gotten the message on the importance of rebundling jobs, and has developed a strong manager pipeline as a key part of that effort. Through its Walmart Academy, Walmart provides both classroom training and on-the-job coaching to its associates, with the goal of moving them into supervisory and management positions.[4] In addition, Walmart invested more than $1 billion so that it can offer free classes and training to its employees in areas like technology and health and wellness. The idea is to anticipate what future skills the company will need.[5] Walmart has also created a talent marketplace to develop careers within the company.

If employees end up getting jobs outside the company as a result of its efforts, that's fine too, says Lorraine Stomski, senior vice president of enterprise leadership and learning at Walmart. She says that because of its large footprint the company has adopted a "regenerative" approach that looks at the value it offers not only within the company but to the community and to society. Its free tuition program called Live Better U is "a huge pillar in our regenerative approach," Stomski said on a Harvard Business School podcast.[6] So even if people leave Walmart after being upskilled, "they're going to be prepared for the future of work."

After completing degree and certificate programs, former cashiers at Walmart have been able to move into jobs as cybersecurity experts and pharmacists, for example. The associates also receive credit for relevant on-the-job experience. The foundation of these efforts is a good manager, said Stomski. The manager is "the person that believes in you—that sees you can do more than what you're doing," she said on the podcast.

"Your role as a manager, as a supervisor, is in service to your associates," Stomski said. "It's to coach them, it's to grow them, it's to build their talent. That translates to how the store operates."

In recognition of the manager's importance, Walmart also started the College2Career program, in which recent college graduates receive classroom and hands-on training and individual coaching.[7] Upon completion of the program, the participants can apply for a job as an "emerging coach" at a starting annual salary of $65,000. From there, they have the opportunity to become store managers, and command six-figure salaries, in just a few years.

A Call to All Industries

Retail isn't the only industry experiencing this shift. If their organizations are to remain competitive, leaders in just about all industries will need to put intelligent thought into rebundling decisions. Banking executives will probably need to lay off some of their tellers, but could some of those tellers be moved to sales or advisory roles? Automated meter readers are taking over the jobs of their human equivalents, but couldn't a percentage of those employees be retrained as technicians rather than losing their jobs?

Many companies foresee automation as enabling the transfer of some tasks now performed by high-skilled workers to lower-skilled ones—and thus preserving more jobs. In doctor's offices, more machines will be able to take over routine tasks like monitoring vitals that physician assistants have long performed. But most likely the physician assistants could then take over some of the jobs that nurses and doctors have long done, such as conducting certain exams and administering vaccines.

Across all industries, workplace automation will increase the need for "workers with finely tuned social and emotional skills—skills that machines are a long way from mastering," according to a McKinsey report.[8] "While some of these skills, such as empathy, are innate, others, such as advanced communication, can be honed and taught." This will be true regardless of whether a job requires specialized training and a college degree.

In general, it's the people without college degrees and who don't have specialized skills whose jobs are most endangered by the relentless advance of technology. Most of the employees at Tara's grocery store—including Walt, Dale, and Rhonda—never went to college. They were grateful for the chance to receive new training that could lead to steady career advancement. And, importantly, Tara was able to give them continual real-time coaching and guidance on their new, more complex roles.

Walt, in particular, needed this help. In his old cashier role, the work literally came to him. While he was stationary behind a cash register, customers stood in his line, and their purchases came sliding down a belt toward him before he scanned them at the cash register.

He was accustomed to that way of working: In the same way, when he played for the band he was stationary behind his drums.

In his new job, Walt was untethered from the register, and at first his new freedom of movement felt disorienting. He needed help from Tara to establish a new way of working, one in which he was often expected to approach customers rather than the other way around. Tara also helped Walt develop a sense of the whole store so he could identify and help solve any problems that might arise. He needed to adopt a new "rhythm" as he traversed the aisles, and Tara helped him do it. This coaching served Walt well in a range of settings, and enabled a type of learning he couldn't have gotten through typical classroom instruction.

Nearly two-thirds of American adults do not have a college degree. Acemoglu, the economist, has estimated that automation is one of the main culprits behind the widening wage gap, particularly among men without college degrees.[9] So the ability of managers to rebundle jobs and provide the right coaching around them has widespread societal and economic implications. This is particularly true as the social responsibility of corporations continues to evolve. It's likely that the thoughtful redeployment of talent will increasingly become a matter of moral obligation.

Managers, More Than Ever

Surprisingly, managers like Tara can rest easier than the people who report to them. We predict that middle managers' ability to redistribute talent will be more important than ever in the new world of work. Their jobs are not as endangered as those who report to them, because their ability to preserve the jobs of others cannot be automated.

A 2020 study by Gartner Inc. predicted that by 2024 technology will replace about 69 percent of the work that managers now perform.[10]

Some cynics who skimmed that news saw it as further evidence that middle managers are no longer needed (if they ever were). But we saw it differently: as a sign that it was time for their jobs, too, to be rebundled and refocused. Helen Poitevin, a vice president at Gartner, noted that "managers often need to spend time filling in forms, updating information and approving workflows. By using AI to automate these tasks, they can spend less time managing transactions and can invest more time on learning, performance management and goal setting."

When Tara first started as a manager, she was often chained to her computer dealing with schedules, payroll, and budgets. A true people person, she hadn't gone into retail to work with numbers and charts. She much preferred to be out on the floor, monitoring her employees' interactions with customers, redirecting them to prevent bottlenecks, and making sure they kept products attractively stocked and displayed. Instead, she frequently found herself stuck in her office filling out Excel sheets. She knew some of her workers were struggling, but she just didn't have the time to coach them so they could improve.

Once many of Tara's daily tasks were automated—and others altogether eliminated—she could turn more of her attention to matching her employees' abilities with the work that automation and technology were unable to do. And she could also pay closer attention to their personal struggles and needs. This was particularly critical during the pandemic as workers juggled caregiving, homeschooling, and increasingly, mental health challenges.

By the time the pandemic eased, Tara's routine reporting tasks had mostly been automated. In effect, Tara's own job had undergone a rebundling. She was now able to spend most of her time coaching, developing, and just being there for her direct reports. And she saved her company money in the process, because in most cases it is much more expensive to hire a brand-new employee than to retrain and develop a current one.

Tara could also focus on areas that she knew were important to her team members. For example, hourly workers wanted reliability and advance notice in their schedules. Pre-automation, Tara raced to get the schedule out a few days in advance, making employees feel like they had little control over when they worked. Now, Tara was able to focus on what mattered for her employees—and that included having schedules published three weeks out.

Insuring Job Security

We have been heartened to see how the rebundling of jobs has played out in the insurance industry, particularly in the case of claims adjusters.

For years, whenever a car accident occurred, claims adjusters would examine the damage in person and fill out reports. But now that cellphones have become ubiquitous, the people involved in the accident can take photos of the damage themselves. And because millions of these photos now exist, artificial intelligence can analyze them and generate detailed reports on claims.

The inexorable march of technology might have meant the end of Maria's forty-year career at one insurance company if not for the rebundling of her job, with the help of her manager.

Maria had never intended to work in the insurance industry. After high school she wanted to be a professional photographer, but she was never able to find enough work to support herself, so with her savings near zero she decided to look through the classified ads for a full-time job. She was attracted to an ad seeking an insurance adjuster because it listed taking photos as part of the work. Even though the photos were of wrecked cars that had to be towed to a body shop, it was still photography.

Maria wouldn't wish a car accident on anyone, but she was glad she could be there after the fact. With her crisp yet reassuring manner, she helped soothe people during a distressing situation in their lives. She also saw all sorts of accidents, from rear-end collisions to no-one-at-fault situations where debris had fallen on the roadway. In the space of six months she was called to multiple accidents at the same curve of highway, which made her realize that its design severely restricted driver visibility. She notified the highway department, and that section was eventually redesigned.

Decades into her job, though, Maria found herself being called to fewer and fewer body shops for in-person damage reviews. Almost everybody had a cell phone at that point, and she could remotely verify the damage estimates from the body shop's uploaded photos. Then, bit by bit, technology began to remove even the report taking and estimating that had been part of her job. It was dispiriting to see this happen, and her time in the office dragged.

Then one day her manager, Ken, came by and said, "Maria, how would you like to start selling auto insurance?" Her first response was to burst out laughing. Her? A saleswoman? But the executives at the insurance headquarters had asked the same set of questions that many other companies are asking, boiled down to the three we identified above: In light of changing customer demand, what can technology do? What can machines do? And finally, what's left for humans to do?

In this case, senior leadership realized that because of their on-the-ground knowledge of thousands of accidents, claims adjusters might be able to successfully sell insurance. After all, who better to describe the mayhem that customers need protection from than a person who has reviewed literally thousands of claims? Of course, not every insurance adjuster would be a great fit for sales. But as it turned out, many of them were.

Ken got the word from senior executives that they would like to have a subset of adjusters move into sales as part of a broader rebundling of jobs. Maria was skeptical at first, being an introvert who thought the best salespeople had to be outgoing, pushy, and insincere. But then she discovered something: When you've seen your product in action and can persuade people of its value, working in sales can be immensely rewarding—and lucrative. Before she retired with forty years of service, she spent three years as one of the top salespeople in her region.

The Employee Value Proposition

Ken was able to convince Maria to give sales a try by presenting her new role in the form of an employee value proposition: In short, he connected her strengths and abilities with a job that he knew would align with her interests and sense of purpose. Maria had seen how devastating accidents could be for people without insurance and felt she was truly doing good by setting people up with the right policies for their situation.

In the same way, Tara at the grocery store persuaded Walt to make the leap from being a cashier to taking on a more wide-ranging customer service role. She explained that in his new role, his interactions would be more varied, interesting, and personal. And that is exactly what happened. Walt loved dealing with customers in his new job. His genuine interest in their lives helped him establish a rapport with them that led to an uptick in repeat business.

According to McKinsey research, 85 percent of executives feel that their work holds purpose, while only 15 percent of frontline workers feel the same.[11] If leaders want to prevent disruptive and expensive attrition at their companies, they would do well to concentrate on purpose. Even the most seemingly unskilled jobs can be filled with purpose if they are repackaged and redefined in the right way. Managers are in the best position to help frontline employees feel their purpose at work. The way Tara presented the value of Walt's rebundled job to him is a case in point.

For employees not planning to retire anytime soon, middle managers can also stress how a new job will aid in career development, preferably inside but perhaps outside the company. In Walt's new position, he acquired a host of valuable and transferrable new skills, including selling techniques and in-depth product knowledge—although how much that will help him if his band makes it big is questionable.

Most important, both Walt and Maria felt valued by their managers for their contributions. In looking at the reasons behind the Great Resignation, not feeling valued was a core driver of people leaving their employer, often without another job in hand.

Decades ago, when a company needed to cut costs, the prevailing wisdom was that new processes would become ever more machine-like and require less management intervention. With the help of management consultancies, McKinsey included, reductions across departments were often achieved through a combination of process redesign and deep cuts to middle management. Workers other than top talent were viewed as fungible (talk about not feeling valued!). In carrying out, say, a 15 to 20 percent head count reduction, leaders gave less thought to the skills of individual workers who might be able to stay on in new roles, and more thought to achieving a numerical target. This was a waste of both money and human ability.

These days, even if a cost-cutting effort might involve eliminating 30 to 50 percent of the work now performed by humans, it is hoped that it would not lead to a corresponding number of lost jobs. Rather, executives and middle managers can clarify which tasks people are able to do *alongside* technology and machines to better serve customers and internal clients. And because the remaining work is more human, the management of that work needs to be more human, too.

And so, even as Just Walk Out technology and self-checkout machines bypass human cashiers, the need to provide a pleasant and helpful customer experience via an actual person grows. And as automation takes over much of the claims adjuster's job, the demand for personalized sales and service leads to new job openings.

When it comes to rebundling, senior leaders can empower their middle managers to be at the center of the action. Only middle managers are the ones who can match the right workers to the right jobs, with the help of training and coaching. And only they are in the position to align meaning and purpose to the kinds of jobs that a machine couldn't possibly do.

 **TAKEAWAYS**

Rethinking the Role of the Middle

The challenge: As automation takes over more of the tasks formerly done by people, more people are in danger of losing their jobs, or being redeployed to the wrong jobs.

Why middle managers are key to meeting the challenge: Middle managers are the ones who can tease out what technology is best able to do; what machines can best do; and what remains for humans to do. Then, knowing the unique capabilities of their employees, they can rebundle— and thereby save—jobs so that they fit the new needs of the workplace.

What senior leaders can do to help: Senior leaders can work to rebundle the jobs of their managers before the managers themselves rebundle the jobs of their reports. Taking away the administrivia and individual contributor work that burdens so many of them will give managers the time and space to thoughtfully reimagine the new world of work.

CHAPTER 5

Winning the Twenty-First Century War for Talent

From Transactions to Interactions

Why did Julia, a software engineer with highly marketable skills, accept a job with one investment firm over another? It wasn't mainly the salary or the benefits. It was the fact that Ken, the hiring manager at one of the firms, understood that Julia cared less about money than about meaning, belonging, and identity. It's a message that some companies still need to absorb. If they don't, they will miss out on recruiting and retaining the highest-caliber workers.

David, the hiring manager at the other firm, had not yet understood that the hiring equation had changed when he interviewed Julia. Still, he could tell that something was off when he was interviewing her.

Julia was just a few years out of college. Having failed to find anyone for the position for three long months, David's company had just reduced the years of experience that were required for the role. David was sure Julia would jump at the six-figure salary, which was almost twice what it had been just a few years ago. Plus, Julia would get four weeks of vacation and be allowed to work from home two days a week, just like the other IT employees.

The interview started out normally enough, with David asking her about her previous experience, and Julia telling him about her last job at a large insurance firm. She was intelligent and personable. There was one red flag: She'd been unemployed for the last six months. David wondered what *that* was about, because jobs in her field were plentiful. But he decided to let it go. He knew that her skills matched the job to a tee thanks to the initial HR screening, and he was in a hurry. As he prepared to wrap up the interview, though, something strange happened: Julia started interviewing *him*.

"I like that you're offering two days of remote work," she said, "but would you ever consider allowing someone to work three or four days a week from home as long as their performance was the same?"

David was momentarily tongue-tied, and then said, "Well, it's not something we're doing right now, but . . ." Then he trailed off.

"And I'm curious," Julia said. "Do you ever allow job sharing, or let someone work twenty hours a week?"

David tried to hide his surprise. Julia was already—albeit politely—asking if she could come into the office less often and work fewer hours! He would never do something like that before he was even offered the job—or afterward, for that matter. "I'd have to look into that," he said.

"And one other thing," Julia said. "I looked online and didn't see anything about your company pledging to be carbon-neutral by 2050. Is that something you've done, or are planning to do?"

David felt a little confused. Why was this person talking about carbon emissions—worthy as the subject was—during a job interview? Shouldn't she be focusing on salary and benefits?

"I'm not sure, I'll need to check into that too," he said, a little curtly.

After Julia thanked him and left his office, David shook his head. What had just happened here? He still vividly remembered his own interview at the same firm when he was twenty-two. He had been in awe of the manager who motioned him into his muted, carpeted office. The manager, wearing a crisp suit and tie, explained that David would need to work sixty hours a week or more in his entry-level job, and with just two weeks of vacation, but it would be worth it.

David blanched when he learned what the salary was; it would hardly be enough to pay the rent on his shoebox-size apartment on the Upper West Side. But the silver-haired manager assured him that David's pay would rise steadily if he worked hard and proved himself. And when the manager called him with a job offer a few days later, David was proud and grateful to accept it.

David wasn't a baby boomer on the verge of retirement; in fact, he was at the very upper end of the millennial generation, having been born in 1981. But he had felt lucky to get a job during the tight labor market of 2002, and to have risen quickly to become a middle manager.

Now David—starting to gray a little himself—was making an excellent salary, with regular bonuses. He was married with two school-age kids and had a big house in Westchester, and he had earned every bit of his success. So it was unsettling that Julia didn't seem to see this job as an amazing opportunity.

He brushed those feelings off, though, and offered her the job—and then was shocked when she turned it down the next day. In a polite email, Julia explained that she had decided to take a job that provided more flexible working options and was more proactive on the environmental and social issues that she cared about.

In recent years, managers like David have felt the ground shift beneath them as they learn that many applicants—especially younger ones—look at their working lives differently from those in decades past. For one thing, they might choose not to take a corporate job at all but rather join a startup (with plenty of equity) or become part of the gig economy by doing flexible contract work. Or they might opt to start their own business, with the entry costs lower than they have ever been. That has significantly narrowed the talent pool for other employers.

When applicants do apply to bigger organizations, they often have the upper hand, especially if they are technical and knowledge workers. More and more, managers are finding that they need to sell themselves to the applicants rather than the other way around.

At the same time, managers are seeing valued employees put in their notice, sometimes without having another job. In 2021, nearly 48 million Americans quit their jobs, the highest number on record.[1] Some of this was because of the pandemic, which led to a period of deep introspection and caused people to question the direction of their lives. But even before then, more people were beginning to want their jobs to be more aligned with their life purpose.

According to research by McKinsey and others, more employees and applicants are seeking the kinds of benefits that simply can't be pinned down with a number. They want to understand how their work fits into the broader organizational strategy and how it aligns with their own individual purpose. They want to feel valued by their company and their manager. They want to be part of a team that is caring, trustworthy, interesting, high-performing, and fun. They want their employer to be clear about their career development. Plus, they want more control over what they do, and more flexibility on where they can do it.

Failing to Diagnose the Problem

Our research has shown that many employers fail to understand why their workers are quitting. In a recent survey, employers theorized that the top three reasons for workers' resignations were compensation, work-life balance, and their physical and emotional health.[2]

FIGURE 5-1

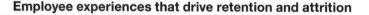

Employee experiences that drive retention and attrition

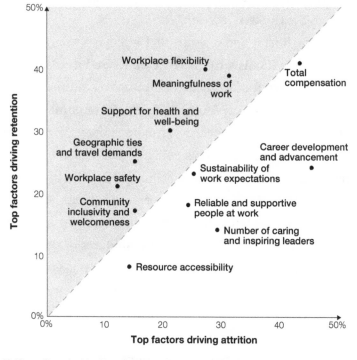

Source: McKinsey Great Attrition Great Attraction Research, April 2022.

Yes, these factors were an issue for workers, but not nearly as much as their employers thought they were (figure 5-1).

Much higher on the list were not feeling valued by their organizations or their managers, and not feeling a sense of belonging at work. "Notably, employees who classified themselves as non-white or multiracial were more likely than their white counterparts to say they had left because they didn't feel they belonged at their companies," according to the research.

Most companies are continuing to throw money at their attrition problems: If I just beat the other company's offer, then Joe will stay with our company instead of making a switch, right? Wrong. When companies understand that their employees, both future and current, want a work environment that is more about interactions and less about transactions, then they will be in position to turn the Great Attrition into the Great Attraction.

What's more, it isn't one size fits all. Employees are reminding us that they are individuals with distinct wants and needs. Think of a health analogy: corporations are attempting to stop the bleeding of attrition by putting a Band-Aid on it, in the form of money. But the Great Attrition can't be healed with more money. Instead, organizations need to diagnose what's going on by conducting an organizational MRI to understand why people are leaving and analyzing the current state of the employee experience. Then, they can bring surgical precision to solving the problem. The analysis could include detailed surveys along with technological analyses of things such as employee interactions and work patterns (McKinsey's own Organizational Health Index is designed to do this).

When it comes to recruiting and retention, it's all about the people. And which person is at the center of making an employee's work meaningful? The middle manager, of course. It's the company that enables the economic exchange. It's the manager who enables the social exchange, at the team level.

Managers who step out of their bubble to connect with team members at a human level make all the difference in how people feel about the organization, and can affect recruitment and retention in ways that HR and the higher-ups can't.

David at the investment firm didn't understand this yet when Julia said she had accepted another job offer. Instead, his competitive instincts kicked in. He emailed her back: Would she tell him the salary they were offering, and give him a chance to counter it?

It really wasn't about the salary, Julia said. It was more that she could see herself fitting in at the other company, and that it connected more closely with her personal values.

A New Life Perspective

Now let's look at the hiring process from Julia's point of view.

As it did for so many, the pandemic altered Julia's outlook on life. Her eighty-eight-year-old grandmother had died of Covid-19, and her mother had become seriously ill from it. Because Julia had some savings, she was able to quit her job at the insurance company so she could spend more time on what mattered: her family and friends. Plus, after long hours at that job, she felt she just needed a break. During her time off, she finally had a chance to binge-watch *Stranger Things*, and she loved taking naps in the afternoon. Instead of working sixty-hour weeks, she spent ten hours a week volunteering for a cause that meant a lot to her: environmental activism. Her time, she realized, was more important to her than money.

After six months, though, Julia's savings were dwindling and she set out to rejoin the workforce. When she interviewed with David, Julia knew she was highly qualified. With skills like hers in high demand, she had five other interviews lined up. She didn't see this final-round interview with David as a chance to get her big break in the business. Rather, she wanted to determine whether this company was a good cultural fit for her. From talking to David, she determined it wasn't.

Instead, Julia took a job with an investment company that specialized in Environmental, Social, and Governance (ESG) funds. Karl, the manager who interviewed Julia, was twenty years older than David and about to retire. But he had seen the writing on the wall. He showed that he was interested in Julia as a person. He made sure the interview was more about the values and priorities of the company, and whether they connected with Julia's own personal values and priorities.

When Julia asked about working remotely, Karl was ready with an answer: "Yes, as long as you're getting the work done, you can work at home as much or as little as you want, although we do like people to come in from time to time for working sessions and to get to know their colleagues."

When she asked about part-time work, Julia liked Karl's answer: "We've started to let some of our people work twenty hours instead of full time, if that fits better into their lives. We would consider that for your job."

Karl sealed the deal by introducing Julia to his team—which David hadn't done. She was impressed by their commitment to environmental and social causes, and their genuine enthusiasm for the work and the company. A few of them cracked some pretty good jokes, too. Maybe she would come into the office more than she thought—they seemed like the kind of people she would like to grab a drink with after work.

Rethinking Recruiting

Larry, the middle manager at the transportation repair company who appeared in chapter 1 (and was not a McKinsey client), has seen the balance of power shift at his company, too. And it has affected his recruiting strategy. As he sees it, his industry is currently "paying the price for the neglect of our most critical asset, which is people."

Because of an industry-wide shortage of workers, his company is now running at just 60 percent capacity. Too many of the repair bays are alarmingly empty. Salaries are already twice what they were five or six years ago, and Larry has experienced the futility of trying to compete on pay alone. Someone else will almost always win if there's a pricing war.

Larry recently made a recruiting video featuring some of the technicians he manages, to be posted online. What he tried to convey in the video: "You're not just going to be a number; we're going to treat you like a person."

In the video, Larry stresses that a bachelor's degree is not the only path to career success—that a skills-based trade like diesel repair can also be rewarding. In on-camera interviews, his technicians talk about why they love the industry—because they're able to take something that was broken and fix it, and get a distressed truck driver back out on the road. "We're connecting that passion and purpose with successful completion of repairs," Larry says.

The video also has the technicians talking about how they work as a team rather than in isolation. The idea is that "I know I can go to my partner and he's going to help me because that's how we operate."

Larry also stresses that the company provides extensive training that can lead to steady upward mobility at the company. He knows if he doesn't make this clear, job applicants will choose other companies over his, or move to other industries entirely. Yes, the growth path will take three to four years, but he outlines exactly how it will occur.

Larry's company is focusing on training its middle managers, too, on things like emotional intelligence and devising more ways to connect with their staff. The goal is for them to stress not just the business model but also the business culture.

A Creative Approach to Diversity

Now add diversity efforts to the recruiting puzzle. Once again, middle managers will be central to the solution—managers like Priya.

Priya faced the same issues most technology companies encounter when aiming to assemble a diverse workforce—where to find qualified recruits with specialized skills and how to entice them to take her offer over others. Her company's recruiters followed the same game plan that counterparts at other companies did: by regularly checking graduates of top schools and scouring LinkedIn and job sites.

And that was the problem. Many more employers sought these candidates than the other way around. Priya's company had the added disadvantage of being headquartered in Lincoln, Nebraska, a nice place to live but one of the whitest cities in America. Convincing tech recruits to locate to the Cornhusker State was an uphill battle.

When your competition's recruiters are exploiting the same avenues to attract the same candidates, your advantage will come from managers. That's exactly what happened at Priya's company. While attending a Women in Tech conference in Atlanta, Priya had an epiphany about how to staff up her team of engineers after she learned one in five tech workers in Atlanta is Black, compared to one in twenty nationally.

Atlanta is also home to Georgia Tech, which serves as a continuous feeder of talent. On the flight home, Priya wrote an email to the CEO proposing that the company target Atlanta for hiring and allow anyone who didn't want to move to Nebraska to work remotely. This was pre-pandemic, before remote work became common, and later her idea seemed prescient. By the time her plane landed, she'd already gotten the green light. The initiative proved so successful that her company soon had enough employees to set up a satellite office in Atlanta and developed plans to replicate the model in other tech hubs.

Priya was demonstrating her belief in a principle that will only become more pronounced in the future: that work needs to go to the people rather than people going to the work. Many companies are opening hubs or satellites in locations with a concentration of talent, instead of expecting the talent to move to them.

Take ClassPass, the app that allows people to take a wide range of fitness classes at different locations. After it moved from New York City to Montana to give its outdoor-loving employees a higher quality of life, the company went looking for cities with more diverse talent pools. It kept its base of operations in Montana but opened a satellite office in Houston.

Retailers including Staples, Best Buy, and Lululemon have set up outposts in Seattle, because it has such a large pool of highly skilled tech workers geared toward the retail industry. Not only is Amazon based in Seattle, but Alibaba and eBay also have a major presence in the city.

Keeping Them on Board

For companies to stay competitive, their managers would be well-advised to take a more active role not only in recruiting talent but in onboarding it, too. According to a study by Gallup, only 12 percent of employees strongly agree that their employer does an excellent job of onboarding new hires.[3] And yet the Society for Human Resources Management found that turnover can reach as much as 50 percent in the first four months for hourly workers, and 50 percent in the first eighteen months for senior external hires.[4]

A prestigious East Coast law firm we worked with learned the hard way that it had seriously neglected its onboarding process. Senior partners insisted that it was a great place to work. And it was—*except* for the fact that new hires received little to no feedback from their managers in the first six months they were there. They felt alone and unappreciated, and they communicated their dissatisfaction to students who were still in law school, who avoided the firm.

Meanwhile, a competing firm that worked its associates much harder boasted much better retention. Why? Because its managers created an active calendar of orientation and casual events that reinforced the feeling that "we're all in this together." Never mind that the guidance they got amounted to, "This place sucks and here's how to deal with it"; knowing that information upfront had a more positive impact compared with the associates at the first firm who got nothing at all.

"Managers shoulder the greatest responsibility for the success of new hires. Ultimately, it's their job to ensure that employees are brought up to speed, developed and supported," according to the Gallup study. "The effectiveness of an onboarding program is largely contingent on the manager's active involvement in the process."

All too often, Gallup says, new employees can feel like victims of a bait-and-switch scheme, with the glowing promises of the recruiting and interviewing process going by the wayside once work actually starts.

Keep in mind, too, that during the upheaval of the pandemic, onboarding may have been minimal or nonexistent. Managers would be wise to take note of the people who were hired during the pandemic and ensure that they retroactively receive the same level of onboarding that in-office employees did.

Here's what managers can do to turn their new hires into long-term employees, according to Gallup:[5]

- Be actively involved and available during each employee's onboarding process.

- Connect what the employees learn during onboarding to their specific role at the company.

- Find ways to connect employees with their new colleagues.

- Clarify how the new employees' work connects with colleagues and the overall organization.

- Make sure employees get the resources, support, and mentoring they need to thrive.

It can take a full year or more for people to fully meet their potential in a new job, Gallup says. So successful onboarding is actually a longer journey than many managers think it is. And really, whenever employees have the upper hand, the journey to retain them can never actually end.

Speaking on a *Harvard Business Review* podcast, Kate Tyler, a manager at Shell, recalled that early in her career she was blindsided when one of her top employees announced that he was leaving to take a job at Facebook: "I was a new supervisor, and I did nothing," she said. "I was surprised by it, and I just let him go. I mean, I look back on that moment—what was I thinking? I didn't call HR. I didn't even look at what was at my disposal."[6]

Now she makes sure to keep a close eye on whether her engineers are motivated and engaged. She has even gone so far as to directly ask them: What would cause you to move to another company tomorrow? She has been surprised at the wide range of answers she receives. For some it's a very specific percentage increase in salary; for others it's finding a job where their daily work is more in line with the company's strategy.

Managers are in an ideal position to understand employees' varied motivations and to make use of this knowledge as a retention tool. They can express this in a form—and even a language—that most resonates with an individual worker.

Gary Chapman introduced the idea of love languages in the early 1990s, noting that romantic partners have different ways of giving and expressing affection. He later adapted these into "languages of appreciation" for the workplace. "If you try to express appreciation in ways that aren't meaningful" he says, "[employees] may not feel valued at all."

The workplace appreciation languages include words of affirmation (providing specific and heartfelt praise for a job well done); quality time (such as a one-on-one lunch or coffee break); acts of service (for example, offering to take over an assignment when an employee is especially busy); and giving tangible gifts (especially gifts that show knowledge of the employee's interests).[7]

A Rush to the Exits

The manager of a game development company in San Francisco realized that her company had dropped the ball on retention when many of her key workers started quitting. This was right after the pandemic eased, and many of her reports—story designers in extremely high demand—were being poached by competitors.

It hurt Sandra to see her employees leave because she was so proud of them. After initially scrambling as the company went fully remote once Covid-19 struck, her team had stepped up. They cut the cycle time for product development in half and introduced an array of social features to their family-friendly mobile products, just as people stuck at home turned en masse to video games for entertainment. With all hands on deck, the company saw its highest-grossing year. Except, Sandra observed, each week there seemed to be fewer hands.

When Sandra raised the issue at a meeting with senior leaders, they were perplexed: Employees received excellent salaries and benefits, and the company had bent over backwards to be flexible about remote work, even when its closest competitor announced that it would soon require everyone to return to the office four days a week.

Maybe that was the problem. Robert, the head of human resources, wondered if the company was being *too* flexible about remote work, creating confusion and perceptions of unfairness since some people's jobs did require that they be in the office at least some of the time.

"What if we require everyone to come into work a minimum of three days a week?" Robert suggested. "That way everyone would feel they were being treated equally."

Sandra knew his proposal would be the wrong move for her teams of story designers, who had labored to develop seamless routines over the past year. Her employees had replaced their commute time with heads-down time. Considering the banner year they had just had, she wasn't sure how they would have done it if they had been fighting San Francisco traffic during their commutes.

In fact, working remotely had pushed her team to formalize ad hoc procedures, which hastened the delivery of creative products with fewer bugs—a point of pride for the team. It would feel like a slap in the face if they received a blanket command to come into the office on pre-mandated days. She knew it would further aggravate the company's retention problem.

In addition, such a policy wouldn't just be a slap in the face to the team—it would also show a lack of respect for Sandra's judgment. Unlike some managers who weren't always available to their teams during the pandemic, Sandra had made sure to set up regular one-on-one Zoom time with her employees. Not only did she ask how their work was going, but she also asked how their lives were going. Everyone had a different story about how the pandemic was affecting them, and Sandra made sure to listen. She learned of the struggles they faced over things like child care, homeschooling, getting sick, and feeling isolated. Based on her deep knowledge of not just the work, but also of her workers, Sandra knew of the trade-offs and sacrifices that the people on her team had made.

As the brass debated its post-pandemic options, Sandra felt uneasy about an unspoken desire that she sensed from some leaders to reassert control over the company's sprawling and diffuse workforce. When the chief operating officer asked, "How do we determine what would justify a team working remotely and what wouldn't?" Sandra spoke up. "You can't," she told him. "Each team has its own rhythm. From where you're sitting, you won't see the differences."

Sandra argued that because dynamics and circumstances vary across groups, the solutions to building a hybrid work environment needed to remain flexible, nuanced, and team-based—not a one-size-fits-all edict. Her message to her bosses: "Trust your managers to make that decision. Hold them accountable for the outcomes they are expected to deliver."

A New Plan for a New Era

Desperate to stanch the effects of rising attrition, the top bosses decided to listen to Sandra. They instructed all the middle managers to craft individualized remote-work plans for their teams. This involved talking to each team member and discovering the demands of their home life, along with their preferred working styles. In addition to individual preferences, Sandra considered the types of work the team did and whether it was best done in person or virtually.

She knew that certain activities were rendered much more effective when done in person—things like highly collaborative and creative work; community building to strengthen connections; and coaching of junior staff. During the pandemic, for example, she had found herself wishing that the game designers could gather in person and go crazy with ideas in meetings, as they used to do. The energy, excitement, and leaps of imagination that occurred in person just couldn't be replicated over Zoom.

Sandra's team needed to operate like a smooth-sailing ship, with each person playing a key role. But many on her team had joined the company during the pandemic, and the personal connections and camaraderie that normally grow organically in the office just didn't exist. Sandra knew she could develop those bonds more quickly at an in-person activity like a retreat, an all-day workshop, or even an escape room.

Sandra always wanted to spend more time with her team—not just on general career development conversations that were fairly conducive to a video call with a cup of coffee in hand, but on real training and apprenticing. That meant things like being in the same room and taking turns at the keyboard to show shortcuts and introduce her new graphic designers to helpful tools.

Importantly, Sandra worked to draw a firm line between the work that should and shouldn't get done in the office. She knew her employees would get frustrated if they weren't focused on doing high-value work when they made the commute into the city. Tasks such as scheduling, program management, and status updates could be done just as effectively from employees' homes as from the office. Similarly, individual contributor work where her staff was working on their separate parts of a design didn't require in-office time.

Sandra also had the foresight to make sure that in-office work policies matched the cadence of the work. At the beginning of a project, the hours were fairly predictable. Mondays were a common day in the office. Wednesdays were generally heads-down days, a time for the team to work on their own deliverables. Sandra often planned a community-building event during those days, like a team lunch or a happy hour. This made coming into the office feel like a high-value use of people's time. On the other days of the week, employees could choose to come into the office or stay home.

As the deadline for a game nears, though, the designers inevitably are forced to work long hours—that's because the release date changes, story lines are altered, bugs appear, or any number of other issues emerge. Burnout is always a peril during these crunch times. During these final-week sprints, it's just not realistic for designers to follow a 9-to-5 schedule. Before the pandemic many of them never went home at all and just tried to grab a few z's under their desks. Needless to say, that was not very comfortable.

So, during final-week sprints, Sandra dropped the in-office requirement, enabling workers to save commute time and grab some sleep in their own beds.

Sandra involved her team members in developing these norms, and they took stock regularly on their new ways of working: What was serving them? What should they change? It wasn't a complete democracy, but her employees did feel valued and supported in both their professional and personal pursuits.

And Sandra was delighted to see that many of her employees decided to come into the office even when it wasn't mandated. She knew that if she created enticements rather than requirements for coming into work, she would be more likely to create a lively and productive in-office environment. So she made sure that she planned voluntary social and training events on non-mandated days. She also asked the company to up its snack game.

Given what they had been through, the team members had become extremely close during the pandemic. Meeting in the office again—and meeting some newer colleagues in person for the first time—was refreshing and rejuvenating. Friendships formed and strengthened, so that most people ended up coming in at least an extra day, and sometimes three or four, to collaborate and just hang out with their colleagues. And it didn't hurt that the gaming company had a very cool office, with all kinds of arcade games, old and new, lining the walls.

Other team leaders, impressed by the consistently high engagement scores on Sandra's team, started to ask questions, and she shared what was working for her. Her biggest piece of advice: "Treat your employees like the grown-ups they are."

After six months, the new strategy started to pay off, and the retention rate at the company improved dramatically. It wasn't just the more flexible work-from-home policies that improved retention: Empowering middle managers to make more decisions about their employees also helped each team establish a unique sense of identity and belonging.

The employees tended to feel more loyal to their individual game franchise and the studio that ran it, rather than the corporation that was in charge of all the franchises. Sandra's team, for example, with its family-friendly games populated by animal characters, had a whole different way of operating from another team that had galactic enemies constantly battling it out in space. By loosening their grip and issuing fewer companywide edicts, senior leaders saw a blossoming of creativity and productivity within each franchise—and gave employees more of a reason to stay.

The leaders also developed a long-overdue appreciation for Sandra, who—although she never told her bosses this—had almost been poached by a rival company herself. Just as Sandra had done with her own employees, her own boss asked what would help her be a better manager. In response to her feedback, they took some administrative tasks off her plate so she had more time to spend with her employees.

The Three Types of Purpose

At the gaming company and beyond, employees have been taking a hard look at the purpose of their lives. More of them want the purpose of their company to align with their career purpose and their individual purpose. We've been surprised to see how few senior leaders understand the value of the three kinds of purpose in recruiting and retaining employees.

Stressing purpose not only prevents people from being poached by other companies. It also lessens the lure people have felt to start their own businesses. Being part of a larger group with a common purpose is a powerful incentive that being a sole proprietor simply cannot match.

According to a McKinsey survey, almost two-thirds of workers based in the United States said the pandemic had caused them to reflect on their life's purpose. Almost half said Covid-19 had caused them to reconsider the kind of work they do. And there was a generational difference in the responses: Millennials were three times more likely to say they were reassessing the role of work in their lives.[8]

When asked if people were living their purpose in their daily work, there was a huge gap between senior leaders and other workers. Upper management was almost eight times more likely than other workers to say that their work holds purpose. That's a problem.

Research has found that people who feel their work has purpose are more productive and inspired than those who don't. There are so many reasons why cultivating a three-layered sense of purpose is a worthwhile endeavor.

The challenge? Each person's purpose takes a unique form, so tailoring it to a company's overall purpose is ideally a ground-level operation. Again, middle managers are the only ones who can accomplish this task.

The middle manager is responsible for deeply understanding the company's purpose—and also for deeply understanding each individual's purpose. The manager brings that to life in coaching conversations.

Some people seek to have a massive impact on society. For others, purpose is aligned to providing for their families. Other people want to make life better every day for the people around them and feel that showing kindness in small ways equates to big purpose. The list goes on and on.

Understanding these differences among employees requires real listening and responsiveness on the part of managers. It may even lead a manager to encourage someone to pursue their purpose elsewhere, for the long-term happiness of both the individual and the team.

The New Meaning of Loyalty

For people like David at the investment firm, loyalty on the job was always a one-way street. The tacit understanding between his employer and him was: "Do what you're told because I'm paying you to do it." Employment was viewed as an economic exchange, and little more. This kind of thinking is a holdover from the Industrial Revolution that just doesn't have a lot of relevance anymore.

After David interviewed Julia, and more people like her, he realized that his thinking had to change. He needed to start demonstrating loyalty to his employees, too. Otherwise they would leave. And Julia and her peers taught him one thing for certain—that the pendulum had swung in favor of the worker. And worker power is on the rise.

Senior leaders need to ask the following questions as they strive to reduce attrition at their companies:[9]

Do we shelter toxic leaders? Take a close look at the teams where attrition is higher than average. Chances are those teams are harboring managers who are failing to support and develop their employees.

Do we have the right people in the right places, especially managers? The most effective middle managers are compassionate and empathetic.

Are our managers checking in on their reports regularly? They can get a sense of the overall workplace "vibe" with both one-on-one sessions and pulse checks.

How strong is our culture? As most companies shift to some kind of hybrid workforce, the way this expresses itself in the company culture necessarily changes. The best managers give careful thought to who is in the office and who is at home, and consider how to forge connections and commonalities among these groups. The new hybrid model is an ideal opportunity to conduct a thorough culture "audit."

Is our work environment transactional? Your best employees will almost always be able to command higher compensation somewhere else. By stressing transactions over relationships, you unthinkingly indicate that their value to you as people just isn't important.

Are our benefits aligned with employee priorities? Realize that family-focused benefits, such as expanding child care and nursing options, may be more important than the more traditional perks like free parking and free tickets to concerts and games for some, while child-free employees may want a completely different set of benefits, such as a workout stipend or access to subsidized dog walkers.

Can we provide the career paths and development opportunities that employees want? Of course, career advancement can mean promoting someone into a more senior role, but it can also mean promoting them *within* the job they already hold.

By answering these questions, and putting middle managers in charge of setting the right course, employers can make their organizations a place where people want to come—and where they want to stay.

⬤ TAKEAWAYS

Rethinking the Role of the Middle

The challenge: With many workers having the upper hand in the labor market, the war for talent is fiercer than ever. Too many employers are responding with overly simplistic and tone-deaf solutions.

Why middle managers are key to meeting the challenge: Only managers can offer the day-to-day sense of purpose, belonging, and identity that many workers crave. And only they can craft the types of tailored—

as opposed to one-size-fits-all—working arrangements that will aid in both recruitment and retention, increase diversity, and result in high-value work.

How senior leaders can help: Executives can resist the urge to exert standardized control from the top. Provided that they have chosen middle managers who are best suited to the role, trained them well, and given them time to focus on their people, they can trust their managers to come up with the recruiting and retention strategies that are right for their teams.

CHAPTER 6

Melding Performance and Purpose

From Infrequent Evaluator to Continuous Coach

All year long, Brianna assumed she was doing a good job, even a great job. But when she went in for her year-end performance review, she discovered that her manager thought otherwise. At that point, Brianna felt blindsided.

Brianna worked in the marketing department of a biotech company that had developed a drug that cured a fatal disease. She deliberately chose a job at a scrappy startup over a large corporation because the work was so exciting and cutting edge.

Brianna loved her work, although sometimes it got pretty chaotic. Some days she almost felt dizzy as she jumped from one project and one email and one meeting to the next. But that's just how startup life was, she figured.

Despite occasionally missing deadlines, Brianna took pride in her work. So when it was time for her evaluation, she wasn't overly concerned. She really didn't interact with her own boss, Zoe, all that much, especially after the office switched to mainly remote work. But wasn't that a good sign? If there were serious problems, she would have heard about them, Brianna reasoned. She was looking forward to the raise and bonus that would kick in after her evaluation.

The meeting in Zoe's office started on a positive note. Zoe was familiar with the "criticism sandwich" method of delivering feedback: start off with some praise, deliver the criticism in the middle, and then soften the blow by ending with another layer of praise.

"Your coworkers really like you, and I appreciate all the effort you put into the Canada campaign," Zoe began.

"Thank you!" Brianna said.

"But . . ."

Brianna stiffened in her chair. But what?

"But it seems you've been having some issues completing projects," Zoe said. "That presentation for the Germany campaign is four weeks overdue."

Brianna bristled a little. "But you know I've also been working on the Canada campaign," she said, trying to keep the defensiveness out of her voice.

"But it's the Germany campaign that's the highest priority right now," Zoe said. "I talked about that in a meeting a few months ago."

Now that Zoe mentioned it, Brianna did vaguely recall that Zoom meeting about the Germany campaign. But there had been five other people in that meeting, and the comment hadn't really stuck in her head. It was so easy for Brianna to get distracted because her husband also worked from home, and during the pandemic they had adopted a very needy rescue dog.

"I'm giving you a rating of three out of five, and a 2 percent raise, and we'll see how you're doing in six months, okay?" Zoe said. "And like I say, we really appreciate all the hard work you've put in."

Brianna walked out of Zoe's office defeated and disappointed. She had been hoping for at least a 5 percent raise, and maybe even 10 percent, plus a bonus and some additional options. This seemed like a punishment.

After Brianna left, Zoe sat alone in her office, feeling bad herself. She knew Brianna was a good worker. Zoe wondered: What could she have done to make this performance evaluation more positive and useful?

A lot, as it turns out. But the fault wasn't mainly Zoe's; it was with Zoe's bosses—and with the company as a whole for not understanding that assessing employee performance is a year-round responsibility, not a calendar-driven exercise. And it's also best viewed as a holistic endeavor that taps into the purpose of each individual employee.

The Power of Purpose

Over and over in this book, we stress the role of purpose in managing people. This is especially important when it comes to evaluating their performance.

In order to truly bring out the best in their employees, the best managers:

- Show how the work ties to the company's purpose.

- Show how the work ties to each individual's purpose.

- Show how the work contributes to corporate goals.

Some parts of the purpose equation are scalable. Through speeches, emails, and companywide meetings, a CEO can make a huge difference by crafting a compelling narrative around a company's purpose.

But a lot of the purpose conversation requires a skilled and thoughtful manager who can drill down to what each employee finds motivating and meaningful.

As our research has shown, companies that make purpose a priority are more likely to retain and recruit top employees, giving them an advantage as employees continue to enjoy the upper hand in the labor market.

It might be helpful to think of purpose as a kind of red thread that makes its way all through an organization, from the CEO's office to every individual workstation. Managers are central to this effort, with purpose affecting how they start their group meetings, how they conduct white-board sessions, how they frame their one-on-ones, and how they engage in numerous other interactions.

It's easier to do this with professional jobs, and harder with support and other basic-skills functions. But the best managers are able to pull it off.

Legend has it that when President Kennedy was touring NASA headquarters in the early 1960s, he came across a janitor holding a broom. After introducing himself, JFK asked the man what he was doing. "I'm helping put a man on the moon, Mr. President," he replied.[1] There had to have been an outstanding manager behind that answer.

Disney calls all the employees of its theme parks "cast members" to give them the sense that they are key players in the guests' experience. Whether the cast members are attraction hosts, ride operators, security guards, characters, or custodians, their managers stress that they can all be a part of "making magic" at the theme parks.[2] This aligns with the company's stated purpose to "entertain, inform and inspire people around the globe through the power of unparalleled storytelling."

We have seen many instances in which a manager's understanding of purpose has lifted an average employee to an excellent one.

Keeping individual purpose in mind, middle managers can focus on coaching their reports, centered on goal-setting. They can link the three forms of purpose to three main questions:

1. What is the goal we are seeking to accomplish?

2. How are we going to measure it?

3. What level do we need to reach?

The reality is that defining the right goals is extremely difficult. One client we served came to realize that its employees were setting inconsistent and relatively easy performance goals. The CEO recognized that to achieve the company's plan of bringing a dramatically higher number of products to market, goal-setting needed a significant overhaul. Employees had to set specific targets to each goal, and they also needed to have a short list of three to five goals. Gone were the days of a laundry list of goals.

To make matters even more complex, goals are often subject to change. At a biotech startup like the one where Brianna works, the market is moving so quickly that goals set at the beginning of the year may well not be relevant by the end of the year. That's why conducting performance reviews once, twice, or even four times a year is not enough. If Zoe had been meeting weekly with Brianna, she could have stressed that the Germany campaign was now on the front burner and given Brianna incremental deadlines. And Zoe would also have realized that Brianna was having trouble prioritizing assignments and needed help with multitasking. She would most likely have understood earlier that Brianna's living situation made it difficult for her to work from home, and that she would have preferred to come into the office more often. As it was, Brianna was left to sink or swim on her own.

Of course, most companies aren't as fast-growing as a biotech startup. But if they're not fast-growing, they're probably fast-changing. Look at car rental companies. They're switching to electric vehicles, and adjusting to a decline in business travel and a rise in leisure trips during the pandemic and now the return of business travel. Or grocery stores: More people are ordering their food online and having it delivered at the curb. Even the steel industry is changing quickly, having to keep up with the latest processing technology and adjusting to Environmental, Social, and Governance requirements. All these changes mean that the nature of the work people do changes, too. And that requires constant coaching.

It's easier and just plain fun to coach employees who are motivated and talented. It's tempting to avoid coaching employees who are having trouble and to abdicate dealing with them to HR.

We saw—and lamented—the effects of managerial absence when the phenomenon of "quiet quitting" came to the fore in 2022. Among a certain set of cynical workers, it became almost trendy to say you were doing only the bare minimum in your job—just enough so you wouldn't get fired. Or, you would test how long you could get paid for sitting in your chair until you did get fired. Some question whether quiet quitting is really, as the term suggests, withdrawing from a role, or whether it is actually about boundary-setting to combat burnout and regain the work-home divide that eroded during the pandemic.

But why had these disengaged employees been allowed to reach this point in the first place? A good middle manager would have been conducting regular check-ins, and made changes to make sure that line was never crossed.

As Bryan put it on a *McKinsey Talks Talent* podcast on quiet quitting: "If managers aren't there to help inspire, if managers aren't there to help lead, if managers aren't there to help follow up, it's a logical extension that an employee might think, 'Is anybody going to notice if I don't do this for a week? Or two weeks? Or, wow, it was three months until somebody had the conversation with me.' At some level that's quiet quitting, but at another level it's just a failure of management."[3]

And as Bill pointed out on the same podcast: "If you're going to trigger apathy, trigger indifference, trigger an attitude like, 'I dare you to catch me,' it's likely your employees have been massively under-led. Because if they weren't being under-led, you'd have caught them much earlier."

The Coaching Connection

Quiet quitting starts growing like a weed when workers feel disconnected from the larger purpose of their work. Only the middle manager is capable of making ongoing connections to the three forms of purpose—not a senior leader several levels up or somebody in accounting or human resources. And middle managers are the ones who can give employees *agency* to improve their performance.

When managers coach their employees, they aren't just offering career development advice. They are also empowering their employees to achieve business goals. One type of coaching is focused on the individual and their capabilities. The other is focused on helping the employee improve business performance.

Four main factors will drive a manager's coaching conversation around meeting specific business goals:

What should the target be? This is normally a numerical goal such as a sales figure, a production increase, a new-customer objective, or a cost reduction. Instead of simply informing the employee of the goal, the manager can set out a proposed target, and then ask for employee input on it.

When can we achieve the target? An employee can offer valuable insight into how realistic the target deadline is in relation to competing priorities and deadlines.

What constraints do we face? The employee can point out any potential obstacles in the form of things like labor shortages, lack of training, budget concerns, competing projects, or supply chain issues.

How can we reduce any risks involved? Given the constraints the employee has identified, the manager can then talk through solutions and alternatives.

In the act of sitting down with their employees and identifying these four factors, managers set up wonderful conversations later around performance. Nothing in a pro forma review can be a surprise if these discussions are happening regularly.

The key here is that employees aren't simply being told what to do; they are treated as partners in getting the work done. And the manager can create major employee buy-in by asking a simple question: How can I help?

These conversations spring from a place of psychological safety that the manager cultivates.[4] This is not easy to do, because it is human nature for an employee to avoid asking questions, presenting concerns, disagreeing, and even suggesting new ideas, says Amy C. Edmondson, who coined the term *psychological safety*.[5] Managers can assure their employees that their candor and vulnerability will help achieve performance goals on both the individual and organizational level, she says.

Seeing the Light

Let's imagine two companies in the lighting manufacturing industry—one of which neglected regular employee coaching, and the other that put a major emphasis on it.

Here's the operations manager at the first company, Brett, talking to his team leader, Paula.

Brett: Wonderful news from the CEO! We just got our first big contract with a hotel. This is huge. It's going to mean a big increase in revenue.

Paula: Oh! That is great news. (Her face falls, but Brett doesn't notice.)

Brett: I said we could deliver in three months. You can pull that off, right?

Paula: How many fixtures are we talking about?

Brett: I think around four hundred. I'll need to check.

Paula: Oh . . . wow. But you know we're down three people. And there's the supply chain issue in China . . .

Brett: I know it's going to be hard. But I've seen you do the impossible before! Just get it done. We're counting on you.

Brett leaves Paula's office before she can say another word.

Paula has been through this before, and she knows there's no point in arguing. And Brett is right; she's pulled off similar feats in the past. So maybe she can do it again. She and her employees put in long hours and superhuman effort, and they do manage to increase production significantly—but not by enough to meet the three-month deadline. The hard work by Paula and her team are no match against an industrywide labor shortage and a seriously disrupted supply chain.

When Paula's performance review comes around, Brett discusses the fact that she was unable to meet the deadline. Although Paula knows this is unfair, she doesn't feel free to disagree with Brett. And on some level she can't help taking Brett's criticism to heart. She feels that the failure to meet the hotel contract on time was a personal failure on her part—even though it wasn't.

Now let's look at how a similar conversation played out at a different lighting company—this one between Jack, the operations manager, and Sue, the team leader.

Jack: Hey, Sue! I wanted you to know that we just got a big new contract with a hotel. This will be our first big push outside the residential market. It's a really big deal.

Sue: That's great to hear! (But her face falls a little.)

Jack (noticing): I know this isn't going to be easy. So I wanted to take time to talk this through with you, because I get that it's going to be a challenge.

Sue: So how many fixtures are we talking here?

Jack: Four hundred.
(Sue staggers backward melodramatically.)

Sue: OMG, Jack. And I'm afraid to ask when you said they could be delivered.

Jack: I didn't promise anything yet. I wanted to see what you thought was a realistic timeline.

Sue: Well, you know we're down three people on the line.

Jack: Let me talk to HR and make sure they put top priority on hiring for those positions. If we have to spend more money on job postings, we will.

Sue: And could we maybe bring in some temp people to handle the packaging? That's less skilled work than making the actual fixtures.

Jack: I'll get right on it.

Sue: Thanks. And then there's our supplier. They're really backed up. I don't think they have the capacity right now to handle a big order like this.

Jack: Can you check with them? And if they can't, I know of a few other places that are looking for business. They're newer, but they're good.

Sue: Great. I'll let you know.

Jack: But you know we still have the supply chain problem.

Sue: Right. We can only get the LED chips from China, and it's so hard to get space on those container ships.

Jack: I know, I know. Tell you what, let me see if I can arrange for air shipping of those chips. It's more expensive but I think I can get a fairly good bulk rate considering the size of the order. Given that this is our first hotel contract, I think it's worth it.

Sue: That would make a big difference.

Jack: So, if I can get more help for you on the line, and sign up a few more suppliers, and arrange for air shipment of the chips, when do you think you could produce the four hundred fixtures?

Sue: I'll need to do some calculations to be sure, but I'm thinking we could pull that off in roughly six months.

Jack: Great! I'll be in touch. Let me know if you have any other concerns or suggestions.

Notice how Jack made Sue an equal partner in the conversation, how he considered her input, and how he offered concrete solutions to the problems she foresaw. In this way, Sue was able to meet the deadline and pave the way for more hotel contracts at the company.

Taking the employee's agency out of the performance conversation can have people feeling and acting like robots. Part of the reason corporations are experiencing an attrition crisis is because people are being told what to do without being asked for their input. True leaders want employees who are engaged with both their heads and their hearts, and that means cultivating employees who do much more than simply follow orders. Employees want their managers to see them, to know them, and to know what really matters to them.

The frequency and length of these coaching conversations is best driven by the cadence of the work, not the calendar. The calendar is arbitrary. Work is not. There may be times when a department is furiously working to finish a project, and other times when it is in a quieter, information-gathering stage. Sometimes a manager will need to talk one-on-one with an employee every single day. Other times a month may go by before a conversation is necessary.

So how can senior leaders move from theory to execution in improving worker performance? As always, the talent of management is the management of talent. Just as effective middle managers coach and develop their reports, so do effective senior leaders coach and develop their middle managers.

Successful managers are made, not born. Sure, some people have an innate talent for inspiring people, but effective management is a skill, and like most skills it can be taught, practiced, and nurtured. In the same way that other professionals, from musicians to writers to chefs, hone their craft, so too can managers develop the necessary competencies. Unfortunately, the vast majority of corporate training dollars go to orientation of new hires, compliance with procedures, and the rollout of new products or systems, with very little spent on actual management development.

I Can't, I Won't, I'm Not Allowed

Simple but powerful training frameworks and practice sessions can help middle managers answer a basic question: Why would a well-intentioned, rational employee do something—or not do something—that is counter to their success?

Often, we have found, the answer comes down to one of three things: "I can't," "I won't," or "I'm not allowed to."[6] It's like an iceberg: One of these mindsets or beliefs tends to lurk beneath a worker's observable, and perhaps confounding, behavior. The manager is the one who can pinpoint where the disconnect lies and work to remedy it.

An employee who says "I can't" do something might be referring to a lack of time, skills, or resources, or a combination of them. Someone who says "I won't" could be afraid they will be punished or ridiculed or lose their social standing if they perform a particular task. Or, the task may conflict with their values, their identity, or their long-term goals. And when a worker says, "I'm not allowed to," then it's time for the manager to take a close look at real and perceived decision rights around a task.

All too frequently, a manager stops asking "why" much too early. As the former Toyota executive Taiichi Ohno famously pointed out, a manager often needs to ask "why" five or more times to really get to the heart of an issue.[7]

For example, if a manager notices that an employee did not bring up the potential risks of a particular project, the first answer to the "why" might be, "I didn't think anyone would listen to me." But as the manager continues to probe, it might become clear that the employee stayed quiet because they were afraid they'd be fired if they identified problems. By getting to the underlying mindsets and beliefs beneath the surface, the manager can implement the right interventions.

FIGURE 6-1

How managers can provide effective feedback

	Manager	Recipient
O bservation	Describe concrete observation	Listen without interrupting
I mpact	Explain effects	Avoid arguing or defending
L istening	Pause and listen for clarifying questions	Probe for understanding
S olutions	Give concrete suggestions or recognition/ encouragement	Acknowledge the feedback and consider whether or how it applies

Source: McKinsey People & Organization Performance Practice.

It is incumbent on a manager to set up regular feedback within the flow of work. Feedback isn't just for when things have gone off the rails. Regular and frequent feedback, balancing strengths with areas for development, helps an employee grow. Giving and receiving feedback is a skill—one that is often underdeveloped. As a result, when it's time to give really hard feedback, a manager can be paralyzed by lack of practice.

When a manager is giving feedback to an employee, we encourage them to adopt some form of the OILS model: observation, impact, listening, and solution (figure 6-1). This should occur with all employees, not just underperforming ones.

First the manager can describe in a factual way what they have observed about the employee's behavior. Then they can factually describe the impact that the behavior has on others. After that, it is important for the manager to listen closely (without interrupting) as the employee reacts and responds to the feedback. Then the manager can acknowledge their point of view and thank the employee for their input. From there, the manager and employee can create a strategy for dealing with the issue.

Let's say there's a manager, Farrah, who has observed that one of her reports, Rhonda, has recently been interrupting clients in meetings. She could start a coaching conversation with a comment like, "Rhonda, can I share an observation? You may not have realized this, but in the client meetings today and last week you interrupted Ray and Alicia several times. I know they appreciate your ideas, but they also didn't have a chance to finish their thoughts about the latest campaign. And so we might have missed out on some important client perspectives. It's just something for you to be aware of for the future."

Crucially, Farrah can now pause and hear what Rhonda has to say about the feedback. Because Rhonda values her clients and wants to be a good employee, it could be something like, "Oh, wow, thank you for pointing that out. I didn't even realize I was doing that. You know what it is: I'm always trying to think one or two steps ahead to move the meeting forward so we don't waste everyone's time. It isn't my intent to cut off people's ideas. I completely understand how it's having that effect, though."

From there, Farrah and Rhonda can come up with a solution: Rhonda, as an example, can make it a point to pause for several seconds and make sure the client has finished speaking before chiming in with her own thoughts.

For the Good of the Team

Managers also benefit from tools and training to gauge the organizational health of their teams. As with individuals, it's far better to catch problems early, and workplace surveys can help with that.

Using internal employee surveys and monitoring external chat boards like Glassdoor can be an effective way to get a "vibe check" from an employee. Armed with information from other sources, a manager can say something like, "I hear that people are concerned about all the recent turnover. What's your take on that?"

After each conversation, managers can ask an employee to make a quick note on the conversation (no more than, say, 280 characters) and send the note in an email or post it on internal company apps that have been developed for just this purpose.

Management training can also include how best to link corporate purpose to individual purpose. We know of one company leader who truly believes in the mission of the company, but when he tries to express it he comes off as a phony, and his employees roll their eyes whenever he talks to them about "making a difference in the world." This poor man just doesn't have much emotional intelligence. Like Michael Scott from *The Office*, he just doesn't know how or when to convey the importance of what the company is doing and his employees' role in it.

Most managers can learn how to link company purpose to individual purpose. But if they continue to do it in a way that sounds patronizing or scripted, it's best if they don't try to do it at all.

Training middle managers to be better coaches can't be one thing among many. It has to be *the* thing that senior leaders stress in the new world of work. It's part of the mindset shift that needs to occur surrounding middle management.

Companies can train managers to offer and receive difficult feedback, to apologize, to listen actively, to check their biases, and to be more thoughtful about how they interact with others. We also suggest that every management development program teach the basics of human psychology and emotional intelligence (EI).

Can emotional intelligence be taught? Research suggests that for many managers, it can be. Daniel Goleman, who popularized the term, has broken EI into four main competencies, all of which managers can be trained to identify and improve on, he says:[8]

Self-awareness: Understanding how your own emotions, along with your strengths and weaknesses, affect your team. This is where 360-degree feedback exercises can be helpful—if at times painful.

Self-management: The ability to control your emotions in stressful situations is an especially important quality in a manager. Research has shown that emotions in the workplace are contagious, and the emotions of a manager—whether positive or negative—can have out-size impact.

Social awareness: The ability to read the emotions of others in the organization. Understanding how these emotions affect team dynamics, and responding to them in an empathetic way, can lift overall performance.

Relationship management: The ability to guide and nurture others, and to resolve conflicts. This includes a willingness to have difficult conversations as problems arise.

A Lesson in Compassion

When compassionate managers check in with their employees, they not only ask "How is the work going?" but "How are *you* doing?" This is not a formality but comes from a place of genuine curiosity and care. Studies show that when employees view their managers as kind and compassionate, they are more loyal. And loyalty, studies further show, leads to better employee performance.

And if the answer to "How are you doing?' is, "My life is falling apart, I'm getting a divorce, my kids are in therapy, and I don't know if I can make my next mortgage payment," compassionate managers don't just nod sympathetically and move on. They attend to their employee's mental health first and foremost.

As one senior leader we know put it: "People have a lot of life going on." If managers are aware of home and/or personal pressures, they may be able to lighten the load before a major crisis occurs.

More than 40 percent of people reported that their mental health declined during the pandemic, according to a survey.[9] And nearly 40 percent reported that no one from work had checked in on them to say, "How are you doing [in the midst of this once-in-a-lifetime frightening and disruptive experience]?" Not once. That should have been the middle manager's responsibility.

It can be embarrassing, even cringeworthy, for managers to talk with employees who bring up issues like depression, anxiety, burnout, grief, loss, loneliness, and addiction. But that has to be a part of a manager's job now—they can't just fob it off to the employee assistance program. Because guess what? In that same survey, the people who felt that no one at work cared about their mental state were much more likely to report a decline in mental health. Checking in—saying "how are you doing?" not generically but with sincerity and empathy—really matters.

This is no longer a nice-to-have in the workplace; it is a must-have, especially among younger workers. When millennials and Generation Z were asked in a survey what they most valued in an employer, most cited "the organization cares about employees' well-being" as their number one priority.

But too many top leaders have failed to get this message. In an article published in the *Harvard Business Review*, Heidi Gardner and Mark Mortensen said that middle managers in particular "feel torn between performance demands from above and calls for compassion from below."[10]

This tension springs from a false belief that performance will suffer if organizations show too much concern for an employee's mental state. In fact, when leaders make employee well-being a priority performance actually improves, especially in the long-term, the authors say.

Even when senior leaders try to show concern for employees, most of them "put on a brave face because they're afraid to show weakness or vulnerability," the authors say. "Top leaders are further handicapped by their own psychology. Research shows that power reduces empathy, which means they identify less with both the frontline employees' challenges and the middle managers who must deal with these issues daily."

Middle managers can take two actions to deal with these opposing demands from above and below, the authors say. First, they can strive to expand their organization's "compassion capacity" so that the onus of responding to their employees' mental health and emotional needs doesn't rest solely on them. And second, they can work to reduce both real and perceived performance demands that are unrealistic.

"One-on-one conversations are ideal for understanding the complexity people face and conveying true compassion," the authors say. It's middle managers who are best equipped to hold those discussions, and to set them alongside work-related goals.

David Rock, a cofounder of the Neuroleadership Institute, notes that these conversations need to come with some kind of suggested action on the part of the manager:

> If we recognize someone's distress and successfully understand why they feel that way, but fail to do anything about it, we have offered sympathy. Sympathy without action is akin to telling someone: "I understand what you're saying, and even though I wouldn't feel that way, I can see why you do, and I'm sorry you feel that way." There is a cognitive understanding of the impasse, but neither person ends up feeling great about the result.

But if you go the extra step to take action that's meaningful to the person in distress, that's compassion—a gift that comes with abundant, unexpected benefits.[11]

He gives the example of an employee who has just experienced a death in the family. Instead of simply offering a statement of sympathy a compassionate manager might "change the statement to a question: 'I understand this must be difficult for you. I have covered your shifts for you today. Would time off, or uninterrupted work without meetings for a bit be helpful, or is there something more specific I can do to help?'"

Showing this kind of compassion, along with offering concrete help, is part of a holistic view of the employee that will redound to the organization in ways that build loyalty and improve performance.

A Better Conversation

Now let's return to Zoe and Brianna. After the performance review where Brianna received only a 2 percent raise, Zoe went to the CEO of the company and told her about what happened. The CEO, Delia, had been getting a few similar reports from other managers, and at that point she knew something needed to change.

The company was ten years old, and in that time it had soared from five employees in a shared lab space to seven hundred employees and a $10 billion valuation, and now it had its own building on a biotech campus. For a few years, the company hadn't had a middle manager layer at all, and when it did start adding managers it did so piecemeal. It moved willing internal candidates—like Zoe, who had started as a digital marketing specialist—into the role.

But Zoe and the other newly minted middle managers hadn't had any management training. So they stumbled through performance reviews, relying on concepts like the criticism sandwich from a random management book to get them through.

Delia realized that she needed to do something—and fast. Even though she wanted to push ahead on projects that were more directly related to drug development, she knew she had to slow down and take time to focus on her middle managers.

She enrolled her managers in a training program that emphasized conveying purpose, how to give feedback effectively, how to help employees set goals, and how to develop emotional intelligence.

Zoe emerged from the program with new ideas on how to improve her employees' performance—starting with regular coaching sessions. She started scheduling weekly one-on-one meetings with Brianna, where they reviewed Brianna's current projects and helped her prioritize them.

A recent coaching conversation went like this:

> *Zoe:* So, how are you doing, Brianna? I know last time we talked you mentioned some health issues you were having. How are you doing?

> *Brianna:* Oh, I'm doing much better. The doctors put me on a new medication, and it's working. Thanks for asking.

> *Zoe:* I'm glad to hear that. And how are you feeling about working from home? Are you good with coming in two days a week or do you think it needs an adjustment?

> *Brianna:* You know, with my husband working from home and my crazy dog, it can be hard to concentrate. I think I might want to come in more often.

> *Zoe:* That's just fine! We'd be happy to see you here more often. You know, I've been getting a sense that people feel like they have to stick with the same number of days every week. Is that your impression?

> *Brianna:* Well, yeah. Delia kind of implied that in her last email.

Zoe: I know, she was concerned about that. But she just wanted to get a rough idea of people's plans. There's enough space here so people can come in as much as they want.

Brianna: That's good to know.

Zoe: Now, let's talk about what you're working on. Last time we talked about getting those marketing materials for France by the end of next month. How are you coming with that?

Brianna: It was going really well until I read through the latest marketing report. There was a lot of technical language in it that I just couldn't follow.

Zoe: I'm glad you pointed that out, because I've heard that from a few other people. I think it needs to be rewritten. Let me get on that right away. That needs to be first priority.

Brianna: But what about the new Italy marketing campaign? I'm supposed to start working on that, too.

Zoe: That can wait. I'll put Pilar on that instead. You need to concentrate on Germany because those materials have been completed. The sooner we can start selling in Germany, the sooner people with this disease can start being cured.

Zoe: Anything else on your mind?

Brianna: Well . . .

Zoe: Go ahead, you can tell me.

Brianna: It's Bob. I keep asking him for that report on the trials, but I haven't gotten it yet.

Zoe (rolls her eyes)*:* Oh, Bob. I'll talk to him about that.

After her conversation with Zoe, Brianna felt seen and appreciated, as both an employee and a person. With her goals, priorities, and obstacles clarified, Brianna's performance showed measurable improvement. Her next yearly performance resulted in a much bigger raise—plus a bonus—and it had no unpleasant surprises.

 **TAKEAWAYS**

Rethinking the Role of the Middle

The challenge: Most organizations link performance evaluations to the calendar rather than considering the cadence and meaning of the work, and how it connects with each employee. This leads to a mental disconnect that prevents employees from improving.

Why middle managers are key to meeting the challenge: Middle managers are in the best position to help define and measure goals and provide the continuous coaching that helps an employee reach a higher level of performance and engagement. Managers are the ones best able to continuously link an employee's individual purpose to the company's purpose and goals. Ongoing conversations naturally blend the "how are you doing" and "why are you doing it" (the link to purpose, and the bigger picture). An annual review focuses more on the "what you did," and there isn't much time to include the "why."

How senior leaders can help: Executives should make sure to communicate a clear and compelling statement of purpose that will resonate with their managers, who can then tailor it to their employees. Senior leaders can also ensure that their managers have ample time and training to offer coaching on a consistent real-time basis.

CHAPTER 7

At the Center of Problem-Solving

From Bureaucrat to Data Detective

Artificial intelligence. Machine learning. Algorithms. The Internet of Things. All of these advances came with a promise: that the data they produced would make organizations vastly more efficient and productive. But as senior leaders enthusiastically invested in these technologies, they failed to appreciate the extent to which people—and especially managers—are needed to make them truly useful.

Executives, managers, and other employees are making myriad mistakes when it comes to data. Some are averse to using it at all, and just go with their gut when making important decisions. Others are enticed by the latest gee-whiz technology, when in actuality tried-and-true strategies like surveys are the best approach. Still others build the wrong assumptions into the data they collect. And some organizations fail to understand and effectively communicate the information that their data scientists are so copiously collecting.

FIGURE 7-1

Employees are more data-savvy at high-performing organizations[a]

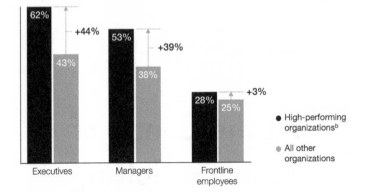

Source: McKinsey QuantumBlack research, 2019.

a. For respondents at high-performing organizations, n = 170; for all other respondents, n = 405.

b. Respondents who said their organizations (a) have had an average annual organic growth rate of 10 percent or more over past three years and (b) have had an average annual growth rate in earnings before interest and taxes of 10 percent or more over past three years.

It has become increasingly clear to us that the neglect and misuse of data has put many organizations at a severe disadvantage—and that managers can be at the forefront of solving the problem (figure 7-1).

Relying on the "Obvious" Solution

An oil producer came to realize this the hard way, after a larger-than-normal number of its drillers started quitting.

Time spent drilling on an oil patch is hard, even brutal. Workers spend weeks at a time away from home in a remote location doing heavy, smelly, repetitive work. Normally they have to share sleeping quarters and bathrooms, so privacy is at a premium. These workers know the meaning of the term *cabin fever*.

The executives at the oil producer had a deep respect for their employees who endured these conditions—a respect that started to veer into alarm when the company's drillers began quitting to take similar jobs nearby. It was easy for them to pick and choose employers, because multiple oil producers worked land in the same oil-rich area. The worker could go home for a few weeks, quit their job, and pick up a few weeks later with a brand-new company.

It was getting to the point where productivity was taking a serious hit solely because of a worker shortage. Cal, a VP at the company, gathered a group of senior leaders at headquarters to discuss what to do. Expensive drilling equipment could not continue to remain idle like this.

After a half-hour discussion at the headquarters in Houston, the executives came up with an obvious plan: First, raise the drillers' salaries by 25 percent. And, to give the team a chance to relax and bond, serve them a catered steak dinner once a week. They were sure these solutions were a slam dunk.

But Michael, the manager of the drillers, wasn't so sure. As a former driller himself, he didn't find the executives' solutions to be satisfying. He didn't know exactly what was off, but still, he pushed back. He asked Cal, "Why don't we find out if this is what our guys actually want first?"

The higher-ups were not eager to get caught up in a salary war, so they agreed to conduct the equivalent of a market research survey of the drillers. Basically, it involved surveying workers hanging out at a local watering hole and paying $25 for the drillers to fill out a questionnaire to discuss what was important to them, and what they thought of their current employer along with other employers on the oil patch.

What the company found out was completely unexpected. It turned out that higher salaries were not the drillers' highest priority. Although they certainly wouldn't turn down extra money, many already felt they were being fairly compensated.

So what was making more of them want to leave? Turns out it was two main things. One was that their freezers weren't big enough.

A steak dinner wouldn't have made that much of a difference to these workers. The catered food was just fine. But often the drillers just wanted a taste of something from home. It was frustrating that there wasn't enough room for the food that their spouses had lovingly prepared for them, or that they had made for themselves. Sure, eating that food might come with a dose of homesickness, but it was worth it.

Michael had suspected that this was the case, but he needed the employee survey to confirm it. Once he saw the results, he arranged for more and bigger freezers to be delivered to the workers as soon as possible. He also alerted Cal that this might be an issue at other company locations.

The other reason for the high turnover caught Michael and the executives completely off guard: The workers had a strong perception that their working conditions were unsafe. In actuality, the company had one of the highest safety ratings in the industry. But as it turned out, Michael had not sufficiently emphasized safety in his daily meetings with the workers. Rather, he had talked more about production deadlines. Inadvertently, he was conveying the idea that speed was more important than safety.

So Michael immediately distributed copies of the company's safety inspection reports to all the workers. He also shared the findings with headquarters, and they developed a central hub where all employees, at all sites, could search for safety inspections.

Though Michael's intuition had told him something was wrong, and he knew enough to ask his employees to provide their input, at least part of the data surprised him. And it caused him to change his behavior: He started leading every meeting with a safety briefing, and he set a new general tone that safety was important.

The safety report represented the absence of injury. But to workers, safety was a perception. Michael had to convey to his workers that safety was a habit, not just an outcome.

The story of the oil workers demonstrates something we have seen in many industries: Leaders too often assume they know what their workers want—without bothering to ask them. Instead of harnessing the power of data to solve retention issues, they rely on misguided assumptions. But all too often, their assumptions are wrong.

As our Great Attrition Great Attraction research at McKinsey showed, it's often not compensation that is leading to high turnover. Rather it's more about relational issues, like whether workers feel valued, if they feel that their work has purpose and meaning, whether there are future career development opportunities, and whether their boss is a jerk.[1]

Here's the thing, though: Relational factors can be measured quantitatively.

In the previous two chapters, we talked about the value of listening and responding to employees as individuals. But making broad-based changes requires analytics. Conducting regular surveys is a way for managers to listen and respond to their employees en masse.

Awed by all the capabilities of algorithms and machine learning, managers sometimes forget the power of the employee survey as a way to gather data about employees. As one *Harvard Business Review* article put it, "Surveys are starting to look like diesel trucks collecting dust in the age of electric cars. Who needs a clunky, time-consuming survey where some employees only tell you what you want to hear, and others don't bother to respond at all?" Actually, you do need it, the article asserts.[2]

Scott Judd, the head of People Analytics at Facebook (before it became Meta) and a coauthor of the article, wrote that surveys asking employees how long they planned to stay at the company were twice as accurate in predicting turnover compared with machine-learning forecasts. And a failure to respond was actually a useful indicator in itself: if employees didn't fill out the survey, they were 2.6 times more likely to quit in the next six months, Facebook found.

Facebook also found that employees appreciated how the surveys made them feel heard and gave them a dedicated channel to express their opinions. More than 60 percent of respondents added write-in comments, on an average of five separate topics. Conversely, "not having a regular survey sends a clear message: you don't care about people's opinions," the article said.

Managers and the human resources department can pack a powerful punch through the use of employee surveys. A comprehensive annual employee engagement survey from HR can be augmented by shorter, more frequent "pulse" surveys, which quiz workers on a smaller set of questions. It's like the difference between going in for your annual physical with a full battery of tests versus getting on the scale and getting a blood pressure reading. HR launches the surveys and translates the results, and managers decide how to act on them

On a *Harvard Business Review* podcast, Rachel Spivey, who leads Google's Stay & Thrive program, gave an example of pulse survey questions around hybrid work: "How are you liking working from home? How are you liking your equipment? Now that we're going back to the office, are you excited to go back to the office? What are some of your concerns?"[3]

But, Spivey adds, "I am a big proponent of word of mouth and keeping your ear to the street . . . You can start to see trends before they pop up in the data because we're speaking to employees regularly, we're regularly engaging them. So, even without a big data system, if you speak to the people and use a grassroots approach, you can probably get to some of that data and information as well."

Companies can make good use of cloud-based survey providers like Qualtrics to put the data in the hands of the managers. The managers can quickly fire off a survey to their team, or organizations can set up a standard survey and allow managers or business unit leaders to add a couple of questions that are particularly relevant for their group.

A company called Culture Amp uses "people science" to collect data on the employee experience from a range of sources, including annual surveys, pulse surveys, internal chat boards, and external review sites like Glassdoor. A manager can use this information to hone messages to the team, or to decide what to discuss with employees during one-on-one meetings. But it's important that the surveys are expertly crafted, as they can all too easily be skewed by unintentional biases and a lack of clarity.

Reasons behind Survey Fatigue

Even when an organization embraces surveys that are well designed and carefully worded, we frequently hear from our clients that their employees have started to experience "survey fatigue," to the extent that they stop participating. Often the fatigue is real, but the reasons behind it are not what you might expect.

It's a common assumption that the annoying length and frequency of surveys causes employees to stop filling them out. In fact, as a McKinsey article makes clear, the number one reason for survey fatigue is the belief that the organization will fail to act on the results: "This was often informed by past experiences, where employees had not seen any communications or action as a result of previous surveys."[4]

On the other hand, the opposite holds true: When organizations share the results of surveys and act on them, employees are "much more likely to participate in future surveys—and even respond more favorably."

Senior leaders and managers can work in tandem to ensure that they reap the most benefit from the surveys they conduct. Managers can provide input to ensure that surveys are designed to produce answers that are easy to act on. They can serve as a filter that communicates the results to the front lines of their departments. And managers can participate in creating timely action plans, tailored to their departments, that produce measurable results.

The Hiring Advantage

Data can be an excellent tool to discover what really matters to your employees. It can also be an effective way to find out what qualities and skills you need in your new hires. Just as too many managers rely on their gut to tell them what their employees really want, so do they also use it to choose the best job applicants. And guess what? Their gut tends to tell them to hire people just like them.

That's how Cindy, the manager of a Minnesota fast-food franchise, liked to hire. She just knew that Dan, who interviewed with her for a counter position, would be perfect for the job. He was outgoing and well spoken, and would make a great impression on customers, Cindy thought. The interview went so well, in fact, with the two of them trading stories about their golden retrievers, that Cindy was late for a meeting.

Cindy didn't realize that she had fallen into a common trap: She was hiring people who impressed her and nailed the interview instead of people who would be good at the posted job. In fact, extroverts like her and Dan—the ones who would pass the "Would I want to have a beer with this person?" test with flying colors—are maybe not the kinds of workers you want to have taking orders.

Consider this exchange between Dan and a customer:

> *Dan* (observing customer's Green Bay Packers cap)*:* Wow, you're taking your life in your hands wearing that cap around here!
>
> *Customer* (smiling slightly)*:* I know.

Dan: I'm a Steelers fan myself. From Pittsburgh originally. Don't get as much grief for that here in Minnesota.

Customer: No I suppose not, since they're in a different conference.

Dan: Anyway, what'll you have?

Customer: I'll have the chicken sandwich and a large order of fries.

Dan: You got it! And enjoy the game this Sunday!

The customer standing behind the Green Bay Packers fan was a tad impatient over this exchange, but got over it once Dan started schmoozing with him, too.

But when the first customer picked up his order a few minutes later, he was annoyed to see that he had received a cheeseburger and a small order of fries. Any goodwill over the earlier pleasantries with Dan fizzled as he returned to the counter, his stomach growling. This was not all that uncommon with Dan, who tended to get so caught up in small talk that he was more prone to entering the wrong order than most.

Later, an exhaustive survey revealed that customers of the fast-food chain valued two things above all else: that their order was correct and that they received it quickly. Therefore, a chatty extrovert who tends to get distracted might not be the best hire.

Another manager, Betty, was impressed by a candidate, Juan, who had an entrepreneurial bent, and who seemed to have some good ideas about how to improve the way the restaurant operated. But this, too, turned out to be misguided. In actuality, innovators are usually a poor fit for company-owned chains that need standard operating procedures across restaurants to run efficiently. (Betty decided to keep Juan as an employee, but she firmly instructed him *not* to suggest new ideas during the lunch rush.)

The company eventually determined that it would be better to hire people who, while polite, kept their heads down and kept their focus on the order at hand. These workers derived energy from mastering a well-defined task rather than from chatting with other people.

Before this realization resulted in changing the hiring process, on average only 10 percent of frontline employees matched this high-performing "recipe." Imagine the productivity that was lost during that time. The new hiring strategy also increased retention because employees were happier with jobs that were more suited to them.

How did the company ensure managers hired people with these traits, though? The company had applicants play a series of quick video games, and by tracking their manner of play were able to determine which candidates fit the ideal personality profile. Games like these measure such qualities as perseverance (how long they stick with a challenge before giving up); emotion identification (being able to interpret a variety of facial expressions); and risk aversion (knowing when to stop blowing up a computer balloon before it bursts, as an example).

In one such role-playing game, an applicant is a waiter in a sushi restaurant, and they are measured on a series of data points—from how quickly they are able to identify customers who are annoyed by late orders, to how well they manage the flow of orders, to how accurately they are able to identify the dishes coming from the kitchen.

When managers at the fast-food chain started using these types of games to hire workers, there was soon a corresponding increase in revenues, speed of service, and overall customer satisfaction, as indicated by surveys. It was then that many of the managers had to admit: Maybe using their gut wasn't always the best way to hire.

AI Gone Awry

It's not just people who get hiring decisions wrong. Algorithms can swing wide of the mark, too. No, wait: People are behind those miscalculations, too—the people who program the predictive algorithms. An employee or outside vendor with a computer or data science background might say, "I took machine learning classes, I know how to do this." Then they proceed to bake biases into their programs. And then hiring managers proceed to make faulty decisions based on the faulty algorithms. Managers and data scientists produce better results when they collaborate closely. Algorithms are made to help hiring managers—not replace them.

Joseph B. Fuller, a management professor at Harvard Business School, says inappropriate data usage has hindered opportunities to improve diversity in hiring. For one, automated hiring platforms—powered by algorithms that accept only certain keywords in resumes and cover letters—are locking out whole segments of the population, he says.[5]

Companies have understandably turned to these algorithms as technological advances have led to an unmanageable deluge of job applications. But the filters are so overpowering that they are hiding millions of qualified candidates, many of whom are from diverse and unconventional backgrounds. In addition to people of color, these include caregivers, immigrants, the disabled, people without college degrees, and those with gaps in their employment.

Employers can take a hard look at the assumptions built into their hiring algorithms and work with their data scientists or technology vendors to set up screening and ranking systems that bring these overlooked workers to light. For example, why make knowledge of a specific computer program a required skill when it can be taught once someone is on the job?

If these hidden workers are hired, they are then hindered by short-term metrics surrounding hiring success, such as how costly a new hire is and how long it takes to fill vacancies, Fuller says. Think about it: If the algorithm is making it harder to find these workers, then of course it will take employers longer to find them. So, companies should also base hiring success on longer-term factors such as length of tenure and rates of promotion.

Another algorithm might show a correlation between an employee's location and employee turnover and punctuality. It's reasonable, after all, to assume that people with longer commutes might leave their current jobs sooner in favor of a job closer to home.

As it turns out, though, the algorithm might well give a higher score to applicants in white-majority neighborhoods that have easier access to transportation and are closer to the office, with lower scores going to those who live farther away in Black-majority neighborhoods with poor transportation access.

It might be factually correct that those neighborhoods had higher turnover and late employees, but the data doesn't recognize the structural reasons why that situation existed. In essence the algorithm (or rather, the person who programmed it) is codifying and reinforcing prior discrimination.

To further streamline the hiring process, more organizations are adopting automated video interviews (AVIs), in which a candidate answers AI-generated questions on an interview platform under time constraints. These platforms can measure everything from facial expressions to tone of voice to desirable keywords used (or not used). And they can be unintentionally biased, according to researchers.[6]

In a study of young job seekers (chosen because this age group is most likely to be exposed to AVIs in initial assessments), the researchers found that all of them experienced some level of confusion over why the technology was being used, and how it was going to evaluate them. Because of this, they were more likely to behave in a way that was unnatural to them. They did this to try to "please" the technology, but it was behavior that gave them lower scores.

Overall the job seekers found the technology dehumanizing, and emotionally and mentally exhausting, the researchers found. These perceptions affect "young job seekers from less privileged backgrounds in particular, who might have an accent, use less formal expressions or tone of voice, or even be less confident in how to look professional in front of a camera."

The Errors of Their Ways

Data is also invaluable in improving performance and preventing errors. But again, it can only be useful if it is deployed and analyzed wisely. And the middle manager is uniquely positioned to do this.

Many decisions on employee scheduling are based on accounting principles and outdated time studies rather than on the way people actually want or need to work. We consulted with one manufacturing company that assumed its operations would be more efficient if the employers there worked three twelve-hour shifts per week, plus a four-hour training shift.

Machines were taking over some of the tasks done by these employees, but there was still plenty of work done by humans. The work was exhausting, repetitive, and boring. And in general, people are prone to making mistakes when they're fatigued or bored. These are known as the "dull and dangerous" jobs.

So the supposed efficiency gain the company had sought to achieve was more than offset by the costly effect of errors. Not only that, but the company had not bothered to ask its employees whether they even wanted to work twelve-hour shifts. Executives just assumed they would want the extra day off.

As it turns out, many of the workers would have preferred working an extra day with shorter shifts. And many had long commutes, which wore them out and made them less focused on the job. Eight hours into their shifts, many people started making mistakes.

Data analysis helped uncover leaders' misguided assumptions and helped set the processor and its employees on a healthier path. The middle manager and the team leader worked together to set up the right processes to achieve a better outcome.

Fortunately, automation is taking over many of the dullest aspects of people's jobs—whether they are dangerous or not—and leaving to employees the "human" aspects that make these jobs more interesting and less sleep-inducing.

A case in point is data entry. Workers in this field formerly had to manage almost all the data given to them. Now computers can perform, say, 95 percent of the work on their own, and flag an employee on the 5 percent of the data that might need double-checking and analyzing.

In these more varied and human jobs, the middle manager is less involved in mind-numbing quality control and more focused on coaching employees on how to problem-solve—and how to assist with providing feedback to the algorithm programmers. For both the manager and the person who reports to the manager, the work becomes more elevated, and more interesting.

Trouble at the Doughnut Factory

Thanks to the technology known as the Internet of Things, companies now have access to unparalleled amounts of data. But without a manager to receive, analyze, and, most important, act on the data, it can't do much good.

Sheryl was the longtime manager of a doughnut factory that wasn't achieving its production numbers. Fifteen years earlier if this had happened, she would have been able to collect a certain amount of data on the problem. But the technology the plant had installed back then was much simpler, and it might have taken a month to analyze what was going wrong. In the meantime, Sheryl might have had to rely on educated guesses—along with her gut instincts—to try to solve the problem.

Now, the sensors measuring myriad aspects of the manufacturing process were both much cheaper and far more sophisticated. Plus, they achieved a level of granularity that would have been impossible in the past—and not only that, they did it in real time.

This data gave her information about factors such as:

People: Which employees and team leaders are working at the facility, and when? How long are their shifts, and when are their shift changeovers? What is the experience level of the people on each shift and their performance rating? How many new employees are there and when are they working? Which combinations of people, on which shifts, with how much experience, are outperforming or underperforming the average?

Site: How long has the site been open? When was the site last refurbished? When was the last capital upgrade? What is the Organizational Health Index score of the site?

Products, machines, and parts: What types of doughnuts are being made at this site? What types of machines and parts are used to make them, and when were they last replaced? How often are they maintained? What are the time and temperature variances, and types of oil, used in the machines? When do the machines switch to making a different kind of doughnut?

Suppliers: Who is supplying the ingredients for this site? What countries are the ingredients coming from? Has there been a change of supplier that could affect the composition of the ingredients, and therefore the way the doughnuts form?

After analyzing all of this information, which combined HR data with operations data, Sheryl discovered that the problem was occurring during a production changeover: from glazed doughnuts with a hole in a middle to cream-filled doughnuts with chocolate frosting. And it was only happening during shifts when Bob, one of her newer employees, was working.

As it turned out, the machine involved in making the cream-filled doughnuts was highly specialized and required swapping out a special part; a certain amount of training was required to run the machine. Bob had been out sick the day he was supposed to receive the training, and it had never been rescheduled. The other employees who dealt with the machine had received the proper training and had long experience with the machine, unlike Bob. Ordinarily, Bob's direct supervisor might have been able to diagnose the problem, but he was brand new also, and by a fluke had also not received the training.

As a result of the data she received, Sheryl acted quickly to make changes. She made sure that both Bob and his supervisor were made aware of the issue, and that they both received training on the machine. She also worked to improve the plant's standard operating procedures and record keeping for training on each individual machine and process, so that a similar training gap would not happen again. And she also reported her findings to headquarters. In general, it might be a good idea to avoid pairing a brand-new supervisor with a brand-new employee, she noted.

Sheryl remembered a time fifteen years earlier when she had tried to diagnose a different production problem. Months went by before she realized that it was related to the way ingredients were being used in one of the machines. It had been so frustrating to wonder what was wrong and continually second-guess herself on the cause of the trouble. Now she could resolve problems much more quickly, and her productivity and job satisfaction were much higher.

It's not just at manufacturing plants that managers are using this data. Industries from finance to health care, from agriculture to hospitality, are harnessing the power of data and empowering their managers to deploy it wisely.

Here at McKinsey, our people analytics team has created something called the TLC, short for Team List to Call (and also, tender loving care). As a leader of ten or so teams at a time, one of the authors of this book, Bryan, might not always be able to spot emerging concerns. The TLC program analyzes such inputs as how many hours the team has worked; how team members feel about the impact they are having on a project; their perceptions of how sustainable their workload is; and how engaged they perceive their leaders to be. The program helps discern when something is off balance or not running according to plan, and gives Bryan an early heads-up that he needs to contact a particular team.

Instead of receiving word of a missed milestone or having to wait for the team to proactively come to Bryan with a problem, he receives an early indicator via the TLC and can reach out straight away to get the team back on track. Bryan's first point of call when he gets a TLC alert is always the same: the manager. The manager helps Bryan make sense of the data and also helps determine what to do about it.

The TLC program can help Bryan and the manager match results from recent pulse surveys to data that the HR team possesses. Leveraging all the data points from these resources can bring problems to light much sooner.

Data Myths that Slow Progress

Recent technological gains around workplace data have been stunning, but the human use of data has yet to catch up at many organizations. We see leaders clinging to three major myths:

1. The only data that matters is financial data.

2. Data always tells the truth.

3. Data-driven solutions don't need human input.

Using analytics is all the rage, but at this point the ability to collect data is far outpacing the ability to make sense of it. The demand for data scientists is expected to rise by 36 percent from 2021 to 2031—much higher than the rate for jobs as a whole.[7]

But to what end? "Sometimes I feel we are doing analytics for the sake of doing analytics. We need to have more clarity on what business value we are trying to create," said one senior executive responding to a McKinsey survey on data usage.[8] Senior leaders frequently complain that they are spending vast amounts of money on data analysis while failing to see concrete results from their investment.

Some of the problem stems from what's known as the "last mile" issue—imparting the data in an understandable way to the people who are in a position to act on it. In fact, there is often a huge communication failure between the scientists who collect the data and the executives who ordered it up, according to surveys.

That's why the smartest companies are organizing data science teams to collaborate on harnessing data. A *Harvard Business Review* article states that "a good data science team needs six talents: project management, data wrangling, data analysis, subject expertise, design, and storytelling. The right mix will deliver on the promise of a company's analytics."[9] We believe that middle managers can be at the center of organizing these kinds of cross-functional teams.

McKinsey has advocated the formation of "analytics academies," where employees at all levels receive extensive training in how to collect, analyze, and translate complex data.[10]

As a McKinsey study on algorithms noted, "Using a machine-learning model is more like driving a car than riding an elevator. To get from point A to point B, users cannot simply push a button; they must first learn operating procedures, rules of the road, and safety practices."[11]

We still need humans—and especially managers—to engage with data, to make sure that it's not perpetuating biases and holding back performance. Knowledge generated by managers provides invaluable executive intelligence, but only if they have access to high-quality research and tools, as well as training on how to use them.

TAKEAWAYS

Rethinking the Role of the Middle

The challenge: Too many organizations are neglecting, misusing, and misunderstanding data as they face major changes in the workplace. This is holding back hiring, retention, morale, diversity efforts, and a host of other areas.

Why middle managers are key to meeting the challenge: Middle managers are ideally placed to decide which factors are most important to measure, and then to use and translate the data so that they—and those above and below them—can make the best decisions. And they are best suited to act on those decisions, too.

How senior leaders can help: To create a data-driven culture from the top, executives can ensure that managers receive training to use, interpret, and translate data wisely.

CHAPTER 8

Taking the Lead on Talent Management

From Preservers to Challengers of the Status Quo

In our work with organizations, we have seen some healthy and productive interactions between middle managers and human resource departments. Unfortunately, these have been few and far between. Instead, we have seen relationships that are adversarial, suspicious, patronizing, or nearly nonexistent.

It's common for the managers to blame HR for this state of affairs, and for HR to blame the managers. The truth is, there is fault to be found on both sides, and it largely stems from an ignorance of the new, twenty-first century way in which work must be managed.

To middle managers we say this: Stop expecting HR to perform the talent management role that you were supposed to be performing all along. People leave bad bosses, after all; they don't leave bad HR.

But as a middle manager you do need to have a healthy and collaborative relationship with HR in order to take ownership of—and be accountable for—talent management. Assume that it is up to you to mend or develop your relationship with HR. Otherwise you will keep losing the best talent to the competition.

The reality is that too many people rely on HR for the wrong things. Sometimes managers will complain, "HR can't hire fast enough." But who is supposed to be doing the actual hiring? Generally, it's the very manager who's doing the complaining.

We're familiar with at least a few chief talent officers who spend most of their time dealing with individual performance issues that various managers bring to them. But that's not a scalable model. HR needs to be thinking about building platforms, services, and systems, powered by data, that will meet the needs of many people, not one person. It's the manager who needs to provide continuous individual coaching and address performance issues early on, so that the cases handled by HR are the exception and not the rule.

HR needs to make sure that policies and procedures are consistent and that they reduce risk. But as work becomes ever more dynamic, these rules will require constant reexamination. The hiring playbook from just six months ago might not fit the challenges that a company faces right now.

Future-forward managers, supported by HR, will stay on top of emerging needs and understand how to define and change the rules in an ever-evolving environment. They will take seriously their role as a change agent.

But it can't be a free-for-all. Managers and HR can meet in the middle as they balance the management of talent with the necessity of keeping their organization out of trouble. Senior leaders have an important role too, of course, but only managers have the deep understanding of their individual departments that is needed to perceive gaps between old and new realities and identify which policies no longer work.

An Opportunity Lost

Roxanne, a research manager at a world-renowned university, had a modern-day mindset around hiring. Unlike some managers, she didn't expect HR to serve as a kind of order taker that would magically produce the job candidates to fill her open roles. As a people leader, she knew it was her responsibility to find the right talent.

Roxanne thought she was doing everything right to find someone to fill a highly specialized, and desperately needed, position in the quantum computing field. Initially, it seemed as if only four people in the entire world were qualified for the job. She gamely tried to recruit all of them, but they all turned her down.

Then she did what all good middle managers are supposed to do: she thought outside the box. At first, all the people she had tried to recruit worked for universities. Then she thought to herself: Why? There must be people in industry who have these skills, too.

By going through her network and diving into LinkedIn, she found a quantum specialist at a big investment firm, Pranav, who had all the experience and skills needed for the job. She pumped her fist in the air when Pranav emailed her that he was interested in making a switch.

Roxanne then moved quickly, or what passes for quickly at a large, bureaucratic research institute. The research team signed off on the hire within a month.

And then? The human resource department rejected Pranav because he didn't have a PhD, which was a requirement listed in the job description.

Roxanne was stunned by this turn of events—and angry at HR. She marched over to their offices, which she had barely visited over the last several years, and gave Eva, the director, a piece of her mind.

Eva was likewise upset with Roxanne. Why hadn't Roxanne told HR that she was considering a candidate without a PhD? If she had alerted Eva earlier, then she could have started the process of revising the job description.

"But why do we need to revise the job description when we already found the person we need?" Roxanne asked in frustration.

"How do we justify turning down the people who have already applied for this position with the qualifications that were listed?" Eva said. "And how do we justify the posted salary when you've just removed a major degree requirement? I have to think about these things, you know."

"But you don't understand the skills I'm actually looking for, and how tough the labor market is," Roxanne said. "You boiled down the job description into something that's too formulaic. It doesn't work in the real world."

"Well, maybe if you had explained this to me at the outset, we could have come up with a different job description," Eva said with a touch of asperity.

Once Roxanne and Eva cooled down, they worked together to draw up a new job description wherein a PhD was not required. But because of the administrative approvals required, it took several months for the new description to be officially posted, and then the hiring process had to start all over again. By that time a big technology company, with a much nimbler human resource department, had hired Pranav away.

Roxanne, all too aware of the loss this represented to the university, continued to lay the blame for this debacle on HR. And it's true that Eva could have been proactive about communicating with Roxanne when she drew up the job description.

But Roxanne should have realized that creative recruiting strategies cannot be done in isolation; that's where *she* dropped the ball.

HR is rule-bound for a good reason: to reduce risk and prevent legal problems. Managers are better off working with HR at the very beginning of the hiring process. That way they can ensure that their methods are fully compliant with rules and laws they may not even be aware of—and come to terms with any tensions and trade-offs between the two sides.

What's Really Fair?

This is especially important in diversity efforts, where managers and HR deal sometimes with the issue of equity versus rules-based fair treatment.

For example, it's common to post that a job requires an undergraduate or graduate degree. This requirement is a kind of historical funneling mechanism that helps HR treat all applicants equally. The college degree requirement is a narrowly objective criterion that paints a nice bright line that helps protect the company against legal action. But it is one area where, counterintuitively, HR's policies can work against a broader goal of promoting diversity.

The problem is that college degrees aren't equally allocated across income levels or racial groups. So, in creating a rule designed to create a structured system and protect the company, HR is also disproportionately excluding potentially qualified talent. It is ignoring the systemic bias that prevents people from diverse backgrounds from being able to attend or finish college, and favoring the white, wealthy people whose path to college is much more accessible.

So it's up to the manager to work with HR to come up with rules-compliant ways to level the playing field—in job descriptions and beyond—so that protected classes have a fighting chance in the workforce.

Only 17 percent of Latino adults and 24 percent of Black adults hold a college degree, compared with nearly 33 percent for the population as a whole—which is in itself a small number. A 2022 study by the nonprofit group Opportunity@Work found that qualified workers without college degrees had been shut out of 7.4 million jobs since 2000 because of companies' degree requirements.

"These workers have been displaced from millions of the precise jobs that offer them upward mobility," Papia Debroy, head of research for Opportunity@Work, told the *New York Times*. "It represents a stunning loss for workers and their families."[1]

Managers and HR can work together to challenge the status quo around *all* types of degree requirements. Certainly this is not the case in some professions. Most of us want our physicians to have gone to medical school, for one. But the education system is not the only way—and is often a flawed way—to assess whether someone has the right skills for a job.

McKinsey has learned this lesson over the years. Our employer used to put a heavy emphasis on hiring people with MBAs. But then McKinsey realized that hiring people with a variety of experience, education, and skills would better help it achieve its mission of helping clients improve their performance and in turn retain exceptional and diverse talent. (In fact, just one of our authors, Bill, holds an MBA.)

A Powerful Combination

At its best, HR is about much more than formalizing policies and avoiding risk. It can also be at the forefront of unleashing an organization's value (figure 8-1). When HR works together with top executives and middle managers on talent management, the effect on productivity and performance can be profound. But all involved need to have a firm grasp of four key factors:

Strategy: Senior leaders are responsible for communicating their strategy to both managers and HR: Why are we prioritizing this ef-

FIGURE 8-1

The evolving role of human resources

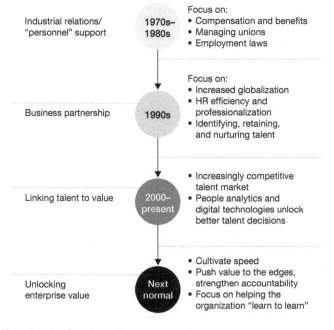

		Focus on:
Industrial relations/ "personnel" support	**1970s– 1980s**	• Compensation and benefits • Managing unions • Employment laws

Focus on:
• Increased globalization
• HR efficiency and professionalization
• Identifying, retaining, and nurturing talent

Business partnership — **1990s**

• Increasingly competitive talent market
• People analytics and digital technologies unlock better talent decisions

Linking talent to value — **2000–present**

• Cultivate speed
• Push value to the edges, strengthen accountability
• Focus on helping the organization "learn to learn"

Unlocking enterprise value — **Next normal**

Source: McKinsey People & Organization Performance Practice.

fort, and how will it make money for us? How might shifts in supply and demand affect our next actions?

A "central brain trust," often consisting of the chief executive, the chief financial officer, and the chief human resource officer, can work together to put people and finances on an equal footing, according to the book *Talent Wins,* written by Dominic Barton, Dennis Carey, and Ram Charan.[2] "Leaders at talent-driven companies are as focused on talent as they are on strategy and finance," they write. "They make talent considerations an integral part of every major strategic decision. They ensure that their own focus on talent is woven into the fabric of the entire company. And they are comfortable leading flattened organizations—often centered around the work of small, empowered teams—built to unleash the talent that will drive outsize value."

The CEO is the vision setter. The CFO allocates capital to fund the vision. The CHRO allocates human capital to ensure that the organization has the right capabilities to make the vision a reality. These top leaders look at talent from a companywide perspective. It's up to managers to apply these companywide concepts to their own units.

Structure: Which groups of people, which business units, and which departments will be involved in executing the new strategy? What will their exact roles be and how will they interact? Where will the work be done?

Too often, managers operate within their own silos, where only their own deliverables and P&Ls are a priority. HR can be invaluable in setting up pathways between business units, but only if HR deeply understands the company's overall strategy and is able to take a system-wide view of defining how the work is done, especially when it comes to cross-functional efforts or work that falls between silos. For example, someone from HR can be the one to say, "I think these people in finance and these people in engineering could be pulled into the project."

HR's role has become increasingly vital as more companies move to an agile structure, where work moves beyond traditional reporting lines, and where groups form, disband, and reform as employees join various projects for a finite amount of time.

HR can be a very effective thought partner in how to design these ad hoc and rapidly shifting teams. But HR is better served if managers are involved every step of the way, because it's their people who will be doing the actual work, in a range of configurations. The complexity of these decisions can be mind-boggling. Collaboration and coordination are essential.

Talent: Managers and HR need to have an early conversation: What knowledge, skills, and attributes does the work require? Do we have the talent internally to fill the roles, and if so, how do we free them up for this work? Are there people internally who we could reskill or upskill to take on these tasks? Or do we need to search for candidates outside the company? If so, how do we find them? Do we hire full-time employees or contractors? Perhaps we should consider acquiring a company that has the worker capabilities we're seeking.

Companies should make sure they are not looking in the same overfished ponds for their outside talent. And as managers become creative in finding new talent, they can communicate with HR on revamping job descriptions before the hiring process begins (as Roxanne at the research institute learned the hard way).

As we have made clear in earlier chapters, it's the workers who hold the power in many job categories. HR can partner with the middle manager in defining the employee value proposition for a candidate who may end up having a choice between several job offers. So when the middle managers end up being interviewed by the candidates rather than the other way around—which is something they should expect by now—they'll have a well-honed answer to some form of the question: Why should I take a job at *your* organization?

When HR and middle managers collaborate in the search for talent, the hiring process can move at a quickened pace. But when the two are not in lockstep, obstacles form and delays occur. And that's when rivals swoop in and pick off the best candidates. In the competition for talent, time is of the essence.

The most forward-thinking companies are redeploying their talent in the same ways that they have always redeployed their financial capital. Research shows that companies that dynamically move their talent around to focus on the highest-priority initiatives outperform their peers. (The same holds true for reallocating financial capital.)

Process: Think of process as establishing the organizational rhythm needed to complete work that is increasingly done in sprints and increments and cycles. How is the work going to flow, and how will it get done? As managers lead the work processes on their own teams, HR can offer advice on the workflow across all teams and make sure it aligns with the company culture and governance.

In an agile context, HR can play a role in redeploying talent across teams once sprints are completed. HR can also determine longer cycle processes for moving talent outside of agile work, be it through rotations or increased visibility for assignments (for example, through an internal talent marketplace that plucks workers from across the organization, generally on a temporary basis).

Let's say a vice president for research at a university has identified an opportunity to attract a major share of the growing federal research dollars in quantum computing, with a focus on health care. She knows that the sophisticated and super-speedy calculations of quantum computers will be able to produce life-saving benefits in areas like advanced medical diagnoses, drug development and delivery, and personalized medicine. Based on the growing available research dollars, and because this area is aligned with the university's strengths and mission, the president and the provost have agreed that this is an opportunity worth pursuing.

It's an exciting prospect, but getting from here to there will be staggeringly complex. The nature of the research is interdisciplinary, requiring collaboration across multiple areas of the university. For this ambitious project the school of computing, the medical school, and the biology department will all need to be involved from the start. Fortunately, the provost is excited to help drive coordination across these academic units.

The research vice president will need the support of HR if her *strategy* is to have any chance of succeeding—because the ability to win grants, and to execute on them, will depend on whether the university can attract and retain research faculty in the highly competitive field of quantum computing.

From the outset, HR will help identify which knowledge, skills, attributes, and experiences are required for the new roles. HR will also help determine market-based compensation for new hires and find creative ways to build the overall value proposition for new employees.

The research vice president's brain trust—including the provost, the administration vice president, and human resources—will be pivotal to determining the *structure* of the work: Does the university create a whole new entity—or even a new building—to handle the research? Or should the research be housed within an existing institute or existing department? Whatever the structure, HR will be critical to determining which positions should be created to support the new structure.

The administration vice president will pivot between the research director and the HR director to make decisions about using and freeing up capital for this massive new push. Decisions about real estate, lab space, lab equipment, and startup funding will all intersect with the human part of the equation: Where will people need and want to work? How will the lab be set up to meet the needs of the incoming faculty? Where can additional sources of funding be tapped to meet startup needs?

After the structure has been established, managers and HR will identify how *talent* is to be found and deployed. This will involve a constant toggling between the macro and the micro. After running the numbers, the brain trust may decide that they can add seventy-five to one hundred researchers to reach the director's goal. Once they receive the funding, they can drill down and find out which types of researchers will be assigned to which particular labs. Ten or fifteen of those researchers might well be under the purview of a single lab manager, who will then work closely with HR and finance to ensure that expenditures and talent acquisition match up based on the lab's needs.

It is a huge advantage if HR and lab managers are in constant communication and on good terms as they decide which current researchers can be moved to the new effort at the end of their current grants. Resentments can build if a valued researcher is pulled away from a different high-priority lab, causing research in another area to languish.

Then there is the all-important hiring push. If managers and HR work together up front to craft real-world job descriptions and qualifications, they can move quickly to find people who are at the exciting nexus of quantum computing and medicine. These people might well be snapped up by a company like IBM (which has made a major push into this field) if the institute allows excessive bureaucracy or lack of communication to gum up the works. And since academics are often married to other academics, the university will probably have to design package hiring deals for couples. That, too, requires cooperation between HR and middle managers to yield the best placements.

Unfortunately, faculty hiring, including hiring of research faculty, often moves at a sluggish pace. Processes designed for annual hiring of tenure-track faculty are not suited for the speed of private-sector hiring in some high-demand fields. The potential for the prestige of working at the university—as well as an opportunity to contribute to the greater good—can help entice researchers to wait longer than normal to see if they have been hired. That said, they will most likely be willing to wait for weeks—not months or years.

Ensuring that candidates move through the hiring process as quickly as possible in an academic environment requires cooperation between HR and managers. As Roxanne learned, any misalignment could result in being forced to start the process over again, which most likely means losing promising candidates.

So, while the strategy for the quantum computing push starts with the president, the provost, and officials in research, administration, and HR, the ultimate execution requires the active involvement of middle managers in research and HR. Without coordination at the manager level, the strategy will come to a standstill because of a failure to attract and coordinate talent.

The institute's hiring process, with input from the middle manager, must be codified and overseen at the macro level by HR. Likewise HR must oversee *processes* related to reporting lines, performance reviews, career development, funding, and budgets. As researchers and other staff from the institute, the medical school, and the biology department band together and then disband, human resources must serve as a kind of wrangler to prevent gaps and redundancies. We'll be honest: this can be boring work at times, but it's also indispensable.

Whether in the nonprofit or for-profit arena, managers can engage in a two-way dialogue with human resources over strategy, structure, talent, and process. HR's job is to serve as coach, strategist, enabler, and problem-solver—all while keeping people out of trouble by making sure the relevant rules and policies are followed. The manager's job is to truly own the people and the people strategy—who they need, who they should hire, and how they develop them.

Things fall apart when HR ends up doing everything, with the manager abdicating their role. Or HR becomes involved too late—with no time to serve as a coach/strategist/enabler—and is simply a rule enforcer at the back end.

The Performance Trap

Just as with recruiting and hiring, managers and HR can work together in dealing with an employee's poor performance. Too often, the two sides work past each other, and make incorrect assumptions about the other's motives and behavior. Let's look at one employee's poor performance at an advertising agency to show how even well-intentioned managers can make an unfortunate situation worse because of their interactions—or lack of them—with HR.

Monica had joined the agency nine months earlier as a media buyer. She came from another ad agency where she had helped to negotiate deals for television and radio advertisements, as well as advertising in print publications. For example, she knew the team at *Vogue* well, and she could make sure that her fashion clients were well positioned in the context of the magazine layout.

However, she was less fluent in the world of programmatic media buying, in which algorithms create real-time pricing to enable purchases across a range of digital platforms. With more and more ad dollars moving into digital, being excellent in digital buying was an essential part of Monica's job.

John, Monica's manager, could have taken the easy way out and failed to provide feedback to Monica on her poor performance. He could have kicked the can to the annual review cycle. But he didn't. He remembered a time in his own career when a job had been a bad fit for him. His manager had avoided talking to him about it, and John had been blindsided when he received a performance improvement plan following his annual review. Frustrated by both the lack of feedback from his manager and the way in which the performance improvement plan was administered in conjunction with HR, John quit his job.

Also, Monica had told John she was going through a contentious divorce with ongoing disagreements over child custody. John's sister, too, had been through a situation like that a few years earlier and he understood what Monica was going through.

So John empathized with Monica. Once he realized that she was struggling, he made sure to hold weekly one-on-one coaching sessions with her. He let her know the areas in which she needed help, and tried to find people to mentor her. He also arranged for Monica to take a class on programmatic advertising.

But all John's efforts proved to be in vain, and after a year Monica still wasn't able to meet the demands of the job. By now, her poor performance was having a demotivating effect on the entire team.

Because John had never really interacted with HR at the agency, he didn't think to mention Monica's underperformance. John did not tell HR about the situation with Monica until he finally realized that she was never going to work out in the position.

After writing up Monica's yearly appraisal, which showed far below average performance, John finally went to Kevin in HR and talked to him about what to do.

Showing him Monica's review, John said, "You can see that she's just not cutting it. I think we need to start taking steps to let her go."

Kevin was understandably annoyed. He assumed that John had done nothing to help Monica until her performance review. "Why didn't you try to coach her instead of just giving her a bad review?"

John immediately became defensive. "I *did* coach her, and I found mentors for her. But I'm coming to the realization that this job just isn't a good fit for her."

"Well, I wish you'd told me about this earlier," Kevin said. "We can't just let her go at this point. We need to put her on a performance improvement plan and send her to training. We need to make sure everyone has a fair shot, and we can't just blindside someone in a review."

Both John and Kevin came out of the conversation with a bad opinion of the other, with John thinking, "I did the best I could," and Kevin thinking, "Why do these advertising execs think they can just fire people without taking the right steps?"

Because of his remit to try to keep the company out of trouble, Kevin was required to send Monica and her manager a host of forms, along with a performance improvement plan, that only made Monica feel worse. John knew that would happen, but at this stage Kevin had no choice. As John had once done, Monica quit her job, feeling humiliated and angry.

Monica's situation could have been handled much more effectively if John had put Kevin in the loop as soon as he realized that she was struggling. It could have been as simple as John going into Kevin's office and saying, "Hey, I just thought you should know, there might be an issue with Monica. It's too early to say for sure, but coming from a magazine background, she's having some trouble learning the new tech tools for ad buying. She has a lot going on in her life right now, so that might be a part of it, but I just wanted to give you a heads-up."

Then Kevin could have asked John for more details and taken notes on the conversation. He also might have been able to suggest training and mentorship opportunities for Monica that John wasn't aware of. This would not have been time-consuming for Kevin; the brunt of the coaching responsibilities would have remained with John. But some kind of early-warning system would have prevented more serious problems down the line.

With this kind of early cooperation, the situation might never have escalated. Monica might have actually improved, or she might have gotten the message sooner that she wasn't a good fit for the job, and left on fairly good terms.

But if the situation had needed to escalate (to a performance improvement plan, for example), it could have happened much more gradually and incrementally, so Monica would not have encountered a cascade of forms from HR right before quitting or getting fired. The paper trail would have been much more low-key.

Kicking the Can to Another Unit

There's another underperforming employee at the advertising conglomerate, and his name is Bob. He works on a support team that looks out for the needs of the umbrella company's biggest clients, with the goal of ensuring that all forms of advertising are integrated and consistent. At their best, people in this role proactively scope out the competition and seek out new creative opportunities. They're also skilled troubleshooters, with the ability to nose out problems before they become emergencies.

Bob doesn't think he's bad at his job. In fact, he thinks he's great at it. He is constantly coming up with multiple advertising design templates that no one asked for, instead of working on one aspect of one high-priority campaign. He's the one who copies five people on an email when only the recipient needed to be notified, and then requests follow-up feedback from all five. At meetings he goes off on tangents that cause his coworkers to clench their jaws as they look down at their phones and doodle furiously on their notepads.

Bob does have some redeeming qualities. He does understand the industry, and he does come up with some clever and creative ideas here and there. When he gets an assignment, he does complete it—eventually.

But when it comes right down to it, Bob is a "complexifier" and an annoyance. Whenever he sets out to complete a major project he manages to turn it into a big, complicated machine that creates more work for everyone.

When Bob came on staff a year earlier, his manager, Edwin, noticed right away that he had performance issues, but he procrastinated on talking to Bob. And then he just couldn't seem to explain things to Bob in a way that led to permanent changes. Talking to him was like playing a game of Whac-a-Mole, with Bob introducing new complexities and tangents and what-ifs into every conversation. Every month Edwin told himself that he just didn't have time to deal with Bob right now.

After a year, though, the client support staff was ready to mutiny, and Edwin knew something needed to be done about Bob. He did not want to go to HR because he feared they would chastise him for waiting so long, and then bury him in forms to fill out. So Edwin did something that had worked for him in past jobs: he "promoted" Bob to a different department. It was a cowardly move that is more common than you might realize, and that may help explain why certain employees (including bosses) are so utterly unsuited to their jobs.

When Edwin saw that a strategist job had opened up at one the firm's other agencies, he told Bob about the opening and encouraged him to apply. Although it was essentially a lateral move, the pay was slightly higher, and Edwin made sure to frame the move as a career progression. Bob was flattered by the suggestion and touched by Edwin's apparent selflessness. Bob duly applied, and to Edwin's relief he was chosen for the job.

Fortunately, Kevin in HR had seen this kind of maneuver before at the company. He wasn't sure if it was happening with Bob's transfer because Edwin had always avoided Kevin. But Kevin was prepared just in case this turned out to be an example of kicking the can to another department.

Kevin always made it a point to work with middle managers to set clear job descriptions and expectations for every new posting. And he also made sure that extensive employee onboarding occurred for both internal and external hires. All too often, it's sink or swim if a current employee transfers to a new department.

Fortunately, Bob's new manager, Aisha, took her job as a coach and career developer seriously. Because she had coordinated with Kevin on the front end to develop a standardized process for internal onboarding in her department, and because she made sure Bob knew from day one what the expectations were for his job, she had fewer problems with him from the start compared with Edwin.

Which isn't to say she didn't have problems. Bob was still Bob, and that meant Bob was something of a handful. The first week into Bob's new job, Aisha picked up on his tendency to complexify tasks and make work for others.

Because Aisha considered coaching to be a core part of her job, she made the time—and her own manager had *given* her the time—to think through how she could explain the specific ways in which Bob was making his work more complicated than it needed to be. She told him, for example, that for a specific client problem that had popped up, it would have been preferable to pick up the phone and talk to one person rather than send an email to five people.

Like the vast majority of workers, Bob actually wanted to be good at his job. And at least having a thin skin was not one of Bob's faults. He listened to Aisha and took her feedback to heart. Yes, he never became one of her top employees. Yes, he was more labor-intensive than a lot of her other reports. But thanks to continuous coaching from Aisha, he became a valued contributor and colleague. By contrast, when Bob worked for Edwin he dragged down the productivity of the entire department. Edwin took the lazy and cowardly way out by avoiding difficult conversations with Bob, and then ultimately fobbing him off onto Aisha without involving human resources at all.

Managers like to call out human resources for saddling them with unnecessary forms and processes. But the fact is, if managers actually do their jobs throughout the year, and keep HR aware of their actions, these processes are not nearly so burdensome. They are more of a summation of what has come before.

Too many people view HR mainly as the place to start a paper trail on the way toward firing someone. And yes, it will always need to perform that role. But we'd like to see a much more expansive view of HR—one that works from the premise that people want to be good at their jobs. Ideally, as they work creatively together, managers and HR will see their goal as helping people unleash their potential and do the work they're meant to do. In this model, HR takes on the role of a talent adviser to the middle manager.

Rethinking the Role of the Middle

The challenge: An obsolete view of human resources is causing the people who work there to be perceived as rule enforcers and paper-trail makers—and the department to be viewed as the place where performance evaluations happen.

Why middle managers are key to meeting the challenge: Managers, in partnership with HR, can take more responsibility for the hiring and career development of employees in their department rather than assuming that HR will take on that role, which it is not equipped to do at the individual level.

How senior leaders can help: Executives can make sure that the top human resource officer is at the table when major strategy decisions are made, and then direct that person to meet with the middle managers who will be responsible for executing the strategy in their units.

CHAPTER 9

Connecting the Work to the People

From Manager of Work to Manager of Inspiration

Olivia was the branch manager of a bank, and every day she thought about quitting.

Olivia loved coaching and developing her team of tellers, loan officers, and office workers, and she enjoyed interacting with the local community. That's what she thought she would mainly be doing when she took the position three years earlier. But lately she had only been able to spend about 20 percent of her time on that part of the job.

The rest of her job—the other 80 percent—Olivia had come to hate. She hated having to be responsible for financial targets. She hated scheduling. She positively despised administrative work. She hadn't yet been able to fill a vacancy for a mortgage loan officer, and so she was forced to do that job once a week, too. It was not something she enjoyed at all.

Olivia knew that the revenue numbers of the branch were dropping, but she couldn't find the energy to turn things around. Except for the days that Olivia spent mostly on coaching—which were few and far between—she felt stressed. Most nights after work, it was all she could do to fix dinner, drink a glass of wine, watch an hour of TV, and then fall into bed.

In her two previous meetings with Abby, her new boss, Olivia had felt obliged to put on a brave face and pretend everything was fine. That's because Abby's predecessor, Barry, had brushed off any mention Olivia made of problems she was having. When Barry told Olivia that another branch manager had moved to a different department at the bank, Barry showed annoyance and appeared to view the man's departure as a betrayal.

For their third meeting, Abby asked Olivia to meet her at headquarters rather than over Zoom. That struck Olivia as a bad sign. Was she about to be fired? In the car, she tried to shrug off that prospect. In a way, it would be a relief, she told herself. After all, now she'd be able to collect unemployment as opposed to if she had simply resigned.

In her office Abby greeted Olivia, and after some initial small talk and general conversation about the bank, she said, "So there's something I wanted to talk to you about."

Here it comes, thought Olivia.

"I'm sure you realize that your branch revenue has been dropping over the last six months," Abby said. "And I'm just wondering if there's anything I should know about. Because you've always been an excellent employee, and your team loves you. So tell me: What's going on?"

Olivia's voice quavered as she finally told the truth: "The thing is . . . I really don't like my job. Well, that's not completely true. I love working with my team, and training them and helping them improve. But all the other stuff . . . it just exhausts me and stresses me out."

Then she made a confession: "Honestly, I've been thinking it might be best if I just quit."

It was scary, but also a relief, for Olivia to finally let it out.

At this, Abby looked alarmed. "The last thing we want to do is lose a valuable employee like you, Olivia," Abby said. "It sounds like this job just isn't a good fit for you. This is a big company. Maybe there's another job here that *would* be a good fit."

Given her previous interactions with Barry, Olivia was surprised to hear this perspective coming from her manager. At that point, Abby asked Olivia to give her a thorough accounting of all the things she did in the course of a week, and to describe which things energized her and which ones left her drained.

After Olivia finished talking, Abby looked off into the distance and said, "Hmmm." It was as if she was doing some kind of calculation in her head.

Finally, she turned back to Olivia. "That's interesting," she said. "From what you're telling me, you get the most energy and fulfillment from interpersonal relationships and helping people grow. And this job just isn't giving you much of that.

"You know," Abby continued. "I just found out that our onboarding department is expanding because the bank is growing so quickly. They're looking for a manager to design and facilitate training programs for new hires. You'd be training new employees in all the facets of our customer service strategy. That's such an important role, because it really helps the bank achieve its overall mission of helping more people achieve their financial goals.

"Is that something you'd be interested in?"

At the mention of this new opportunity, Olivia's face lit up. She asked for more details. When she heard them, Olivia told Abby: "That actually sounds like my dream job."

Six weeks later, thanks to Abby, Olivia had a new job with the bank as a training manager. She was much happier and energized in this job—and with her entire life—because her work was aligned with her strengths and her purpose. Instead of coming home and lying inert on the couch watching TV every night, she actually got back in touch with friends she had neglected, and even joined some dating apps.

How to Avoid Wasting Talent

Here's something many managers tend to forget: People don't like to be bad at their jobs.

When someone is underperforming, it's rarely because they just don't care. It's generally because something is going on in their personal life, or because the job they're doing is not a good fit for them. Waiting for those people to quit, or eventually letting them go, can be a terrible waste of talent.

When managers home in on both individual and corporate purpose—the way Abby did with Olivia—they can often find a way to keep rather than lose a valued worker. In the war for talent, that's a critical skill to have. But it requires a shift in mindset on the part of both senior leaders and middle managers.

At many companies, if a worker leaves one department for another, it's counted as a loss for that department. This results in a territorial attitude that causes managers to want to keep their employees where they are, even if they aren't an ideal fit. Many employees have told us that it is easier to quit and switch to a different company rather than move to a different department, because of this very attitude.

In fact, a territorial mindset—supported by top leaders—was a key reason that Abby had left her job at a different bank. She had become tired of losing talented employees simply because they weren't a good fit in her particular department.

Companies can encourage and celebrate cross-departmental moves that more closely align with an employee's goals and values. Not only do these moves reduce companywide attrition, but they also result in happier employees. In addition, research has shown that when employees feel inspired, they are likely to be more productive.

Fortunately for Olivia, the bank's CEO had recently made it her mission to wipe out the territorial mindset that was causing too many of her workers to leave for competitors. She made sure that managers were rewarded for enabling workers to move across units to jobs that were a better match for them. Abby was hired in part because she naturally saw herself as a talent connector—even if that meant she would lose someone in her own group. Yes, the vacancy in one branch created a short-term hiring headache for Abby. But in solving for the whole rather than the individual parts, she created long-term value for her employer.

Amid all the trauma of Covid-19, we gained a deeper understanding that work and life are intricately connected. To manage one is to manage both. According to a McKinsey survey, almost two-thirds of workers said the pandemic caused them to reflect on their life's purpose. And nearly 50 percent said it caused them to rethink the kind of work they do.[1] And take note: Millennials were much more likely than any other age group to say they were reconsidering the kind of work they do.

Questioning Their Life's Work

Even before Covid-19, more employees were asking, "Does this job work for me? Do I care at all about what I do for a living?" Increasingly, people have been saying, "My work has to be more than a job. It has to fit in with my life's purpose." And if their skills are in demand, they can decide to leave if their job doesn't meet those vital criteria.

Committed managers don't merely interpret messages from on high. They also continually strive to connect and align their company's purpose with their employees' individual purpose. Managers also need to be effective storytellers as they communicate the company's purpose. They are key to creating an environment that employees want to return to, thrive in, and be inspired by.

The best managers interact with their employees as people with full and deep lives, factoring in not only their work but also their hopes, dreams, and values. Otherwise, the best talent will walk out the door. Remember, people leave managers, not companies. It is up to the manager to make the connections between work, workforce, and workplace that drive productivity and also give greater meaning and accommodation to employees' whole lives.

According to a McKinsey survey, 70 percent of employees said that their sense of purpose is defined by their work.[2] But for some people, the purpose of their work is to make enough money—while having enough flexibility—to achieve their purpose *outside* of work (table 9-1). Every moment they spend on the job is a moment they aren't spending, say, with a child, with a parent who needs care, or with an outside creative project. One of us has a colleague with a special needs son— and he is upfront that he is making money to take care of his son in the best possible way.

Or maybe someone's purpose is mainly to have a fun and relaxing life. Those people can still add value to an organization, but not if they're in the wrong job. Chances are they'll be miserable if they have to work sixty-plus hours a week in a high-powered position. They may feel pressured to take such a role if it's offered, when in reality a job that requires fewer hours and responsibilities is a better fit with their life priorities—even if it does come with fewer advancement opportunities and lower pay.

The middle manager is the person best positioned to understand what truly motivates each of their workers to report to work each day, and to tailor each job as much as possible to that purpose. They recognize that this attitude pays off exponentially for both the individual and the organization. This is a far cry from viewing employ-

TABLE 9-1

The importance of purpose in employees' day-to-day lives[a]

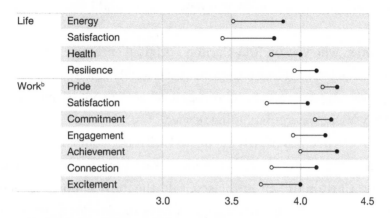

o Respondents who get some purpose from work but want more
● Respondents who get as much purpose from work as they would like
– Score (5 = high, 1 = low). Area shown is limited to scores of 3.0–4.5

Source: McKinsey Individual Purpose survey, August 2020 (n = 1,021).

a. "To what extent is your individual sense of purpose defined by work?" versus "How much of your work needs to be aligned with your purpose?"

b. All the differences shown between the two groups of respondents are statistically significant except for work pride and work commitment, although both are directionally consistent with the other findings.

ees as mere full-time equivalents (FTEs), which implies that they are interchangeable.

Seeing the Whole Person

A company that has long recognized that employees need to be treated as people with unique and whole lives is Ritz-Carlton.

Ritz-Carlton's philosophy toward its workers—captured in the motto "We are ladies and gentlemen serving ladies and gentlemen"— is to get to know them as individuals and to understand how their particular attributes can contribute to the whole. That means constant nurturing on the part of managers.

As Herve Humler, a top executive at Ritz-Carlton, said of his employees in a 2015 Forbes interview: "I want you to be engaged with the customer—you have a brain, you have a heart, and I want you to use them."

Humler, who was on Ritz-Carlton's original executive team in the 1980s, added: "Employee engagement is critical to guest engagement. Employee empowerment and recognition is the core of our culture and how we achieve outstanding service."[3]

This attitude has clearly resonated with the company's managers. In a 2020 interview with *Forbes*, Yael Ron, general manager for Ritz-Carlton in San Francisco, said the most important factor in providing excellent customer service is to "develop your people over time.... Ensure you support your team members with their dreams of growth. Understand that your believing in each of them, and taking part in their journey of development, is what matters. It's a huge gain for all when you as a manager put each of your team members first."[4]

It can seem like a paradox at first, but it's really not: The more you take care to understand workers' individual purpose and values, the more you enable them to achieve the company's overall purpose.

According to a 2021 McKinsey survey, though, most organizations have failed to find "that sweet spot where the 'me' overlaps the 'we.'"[5] Only 44 percent of employees surveyed said their company's purpose was "activated and aligned with them personally." But when companies do achieve that sweet spot, the benefits are substantial: Workers in this group are "more loyal, engaged, and willing to advocate for their company," according to the survey. They are also more likely to say that their company's purpose is having a positive effect on multiple stakeholders: customers, employees, the organization, and society. Not only that, but numerous studies have found that companies that commit to purpose produce superior equity returns on a long-term basis, compared with those that do not.

But this commitment needs to be authentic, not just a public relations exercise. Employees can detect when declarations of purpose are just vague, hollow words with no relation to actual beliefs and deeds. This can breed cynicism, and cynicism is the death knell of inspiration. But when statements of purpose are heartfelt and vividly communicated, their effect is transformative.

Unfortunately, there is a huge "purpose gap" between the C-suite and the front line. A McKinsey survey found that a full 85 percent of executives say they experience purpose in their daily work. This compares with 85 percent of managers and frontline workers who report that they are unsure or disagree that purpose figures into their day-to-day work lives.[6]

It is vital for top leaders to identify and communicate their organization's core values and core purpose, as Jim Collins and Jerry Porras explained in an influential 1996 *Harvard Business Review* article.[7] These endure through time, and they engender a vision that spawns a set of "Big Hairy Audacious Goals" (BHAGs), as the authors call them. BHAGs can require up to thirty years to complete, and senior leaders can craft "vivid descriptions" that inspire employees to achieve them, Collins and Porras assert.

From there, we believe, it's middle managers who inspire their employees to keep these goals alive. They are the translators who keep the goals specific and relevant to their units, from day to day, month to month, and year to year. They are the storytellers who bring the senior leaders' vivid descriptions home to their units. They are the ones who can fill the gaping purpose gap that now exists at most organizations. What could be more important than that?

At McKinsey, whenever Bryan meets with his teams, he likes to have a few personal stories in the back of his head to serve as illustrations and inspiration. And it's perfectly okay if those stories make him look bad. In fact, he recognizes that the negative stories are more riveting.

He likes to tell the engagement managers he leads about a time much earlier in his career when he himself was an engagement manager, and lost sight of a key part of McKinsey's mission: to create an unrivaled environment for exceptional employees. He was ignoring that as he sought to serve another part of McKinsey's mission: to help clients make lasting improvements in their performance.

In reality Bryan wasn't even succeeding at the second mission, because instead of looking at the bigger picture and solving for the long term for a client, he was handling a flood of miniscule requests that never should have been his responsibility. For a long while, though, he acceded to each request, running his team ragged as they worked until 3 a.m. on mountains of minutiae. "May they forgive me," he says now. At that time, "I was a terrible engagement manager."

The saving grace of that experience is that Bryan can now use it as a story to illustrate how he needed to make time each week to step back from his work and see overall patterns as opposed to separate details—and to take actions that served both his employees and the client.

The Return-to-Office Challenge

Aligning work to individual purpose has become even more complex as companies loosen their headquarters model and bring more work to the people rather than people to the work. Wherever work occurs—whether at an office, at home, or somewhere else—the senior-most person in the unit, usually a middle manager, becomes the de facto face of the entire organization.

Workplace shifts accelerated by the pandemic served as an "unfreezing" moment. They allowed organizations to separate themselves from the status quo and fundamentally reimagine where and how work is performed, and how to better align employees with their purpose in the process.

The pandemic offered a once-in-a-lifetime opportunity to remake organizational culture—to actually change the way things run—and to think about how company purpose can be preserved when our ways of working have been permanently altered. Huge leaps in telecommuting technology have made remote work options much more viable for professional workers. For years, remote work failed to make much of a dent in the corporate world. But then came the pandemic. In short order, it became clear that much more work could be done from home than was ever thought possible.

Amid all the trauma of Covid-19, many people found that they actually enjoyed working from home and were more productive as well. Others, though, found that the demands of home life got in the way, and they missed the structure and socialization of the office. Most people felt different ways at different times.

Although many workers reported that they were happy working from home during the pandemic, the sudden shift away from the physical office also exacted a toll on employee mental health and well-being, resulting in higher levels of depression, burnout, and anxiety. In particular, it was hard to establish clear work/life boundaries in a home office setup.

Many forms of virtual collaboration proved to be a success. Others got tripped up by technology that was not up to the task, or by a failure to enact new protocols that would spur equal participation. Some workers received vital coaching and feedback, while others were basically ignored and left to fend for themselves. Whether companies got this right or not was basically down to middle managers.

We saw some companies rise to this opportunity. Many more squandered it, but it's not too late for them to correct course.

It should have been the middle manager's job to integrate a company's on-site and remote workforces—and to involve employees in an ongoing dialogue about how best to do it. But too often, senior leaders decided they knew what was best for everyone. That's what initially happened at the gaming company we described in chapter 5. Post-pandemic, after everyone had been working from home for a while, executives thought it would be most fair to require all workers to come into the office three days a week. Fortunately, a middle manager was able to convince the company to allow her, and other managers at her level, to guide the company's remote work policy toward one of much greater flexibility.

The middle manager realized that a unilateral solution was *not* fair to employees. She understood that decisions about remote work needed to be driven by the work and the workforce first. The *place* where the work occurred needed to be responsive to those factors. In the new world of work, acting as if the workplace matters most causes priorities to be thrown off balance.

And what was actually behind the executive's one-size-fits-all proposal anyway? Most likely it was uneasiness at the idea of losing control. Because if people don't need to come into the office anymore, what's the point of a workplace?

The rapid rise of remote work has brought existential questions like these to the surface. Tim Cook, the CEO of Apple, also initially thought that a three-day-a-week mandate was optimal. He sent out a memo to that effect once the pandemic began to ease. A Slack channel consisting of 2,800 "remote work advocates" rose up in opposition to the memo. In a letter to executives, the group said that the new policy had caused many of their colleagues to quit, and to force employees to choose either their families *or* working for Apple.[8]

"Over the last year we often felt not just unheard, but at times actively ignored," the letter said. "Messages like, 'We know many of you are eager to reconnect in person with your colleagues back in the office,' with no messaging acknowledging that there are directly contradictory feelings amongst us, feels dismissive and invalidating." The company eventually eased its stance on returning to work.

We have seen situations like these play out time and again as companies struggle with their desire to reassert central control while at the same time striving to meet their employees' needs.

It's important to note that more than half of all jobs can only be done remotely for a few hours a week or not at all.[9] Jobs such as operating machinery, using lab equipment, and providing personal care generally can't be done from home. And other jobs—like teaching, counseling, and coaching—can be done remotely in a crisis, but are demonstrably more effective when performed in person. A high share of jobs that can't be performed from home are concentrated in the low-wage end of the spectrum, with the remote-friendly jobs tending to require a college degree and paying higher salaries. A greater share of women and people of color hold these must-work-on-site jobs.

In short, being able to work remotely is a privilege, and it's one that is poised to transform the future of work.

The companies that completely acceded to their employees' demands over remote work scored some early victories, happily accepting new hires who had quit companies trying to enforce a stricter approach. But then the reality of managing a predominantly remote workforce began to set in. And the leaders who had given their workers carte blanche over where they wanted to work began to realize that they were losing touch with their workforce.

It has become clear to us that letting employees do whatever they want to do, wherever and whenever they want to do it, is a recipe for trouble. Employers are within their rights to set guidelines for hybrid work. But these can be nuanced and flexible, with middle managers leading the way.

Senior leaders can empower their middle managers to make more tailored decisions about remote work. The managers are in the best position to answer pivotal questions: Why does this work matter? What is the work that needs to be done? And when and where is the best place to do it?

Some managers are like faucets—they hear an edict from the chief executive and simply relay the message, often without context. They neglect to tailor the message so it's relevant for their teams. The best managers are sense makers, and instead of being faucets they are sieves: they filter through the edicts and get down to their essence as it applies to the people on their teams.

Consider one manager, a former technical engineer who was promoted into management without any formal managerial training. A year and half after the pandemic began, he received word from the CEO that people needed to be back in the office starting in November. One employee asked him, "I am at a vendor's site for business meetings three days this week. Does that count toward my 'in office time?'" The manager appeared flummoxed and responded, "I don't know. I'll need to ask management."

Now look at how a different manager at the same company—one who was trained in people management at her former employer—responded to the news. Her reports asked how the CEO's new directive applied to them, considering the fact that they were frequently traveling to client sites and often worked on the weekends. That manager responded: "Let's focus on getting our work done. We know that sometimes it's best to be in the office so we can collaborate, but other times we need to be heads-down and it's fine to be home during those times. Oh, and by the way, when you're traveling for weeks at a time, that counts as in-office time in my book!"

In the first example, the manager is saying: "I just do what I'm told. You should too." In the second example the manager is indicating: "Let's do what's right for us and the organization."

Just because people can work remotely doesn't mean they always should. Once the pandemic eased, most companies either overcorrected or under-corrected their work-from-home policies for a new, pandemic-altered reality.

The business guru Tom Peters coined the phrase "management by wandering around," which involves taking the pulse of a company simply by walking through the office in an unstructured way. That's much harder to do with a remote workforce.

Managers in a physical office have the option of walking around, noticing body language, eavesdropping, initiating casual conversation, and just generally getting a feel for the place. It's easier to pick up on early signs of unease and say "Hey, let's get a coffee and talk."

With remote work, check-ins are scheduled and everyone is much more prepared for each interaction. The remote workplace seems so much more casual when a coworker's cat suddenly appears on the screen or a cute toddler makes a cameo appearance. But in fact, interactions are much more formal and scripted compared with an office where colleagues physically coexist for eight hours or more a day. Sometimes it's when you let your guard down that the best insights and interactions occur.

It's understandable that senior leaders would want to make hard and fast rules around remote work. But we suggest that instead of mandating office hours, they can trust their managers to build a kind of natural momentum that causes people to *want* and *need* to come into the office. This can be determined by the cadence of the work—and by whether collaboration or individual contributor work is required.

The best managers recognize that physical workplaces can fill a massive social and emotional need. They leverage that reality so that people naturally want to come in to the office rather than being forced to come in during rush hour. Planning lunches, happy hours, and special events can do wonders to cement bonds between coworkers and help them work more productively and purposefully in teams.

Research by Gallup has shown that people who agree with the statement "I have a best friend at work" are much more likely to be productive and engaged at work.[10] According to another survey, by LinkedIn and CensusWide, nearly 50 percent of respondents said friendships with coworkers made them happier, and about half said they remained in touch with former coworkers.[11]

And we know that office romances can be fraught with peril, but the fact remains that in surveys asking how people met their spouse, the answer "through work" almost always turns up in the top five answers.

When, Why, Where, and How

In determining a response to the remote work challenge, middle managers are best equipped to decide on the when, why, and how of collaboration. And those managers can be purposeful about bringing employees together.

We were impressed to see how one of our clients handled the return-to-work challenge. The company clearly stated that remote work was *not* to be considered a benefit—it was simply the way that some of the work got done. At first it was decided that everyone would come in to the office at least two days a week. But with everyone choosing different days, it meant that too many people were spending the whole day just looking at their computer screens and barely interacting with anyone—essentially what they would have done at home. And what was the value in that? Especially considering the long commutes that some employees had to endure.

So the question became: How do we create the highest value for employees when they come into the office? To achieve this goal, one of the senior leaders held a meeting with all the middle managers so that together, and with intention, they could carve out working norms and hours that were most conducive to in-office collaboration.

The senior leader and the managers determined that scheduling an all-hands meeting one day a week was a good forcing mechanism for the full group to gather at the office. Initially the senior leader thought

Tuesday would be the best day for everyone to come in. But on hearing that most of the middle managers had family commitments outside of work that would make their commutes difficult on Tuesday, he changed the in-office day to Wednesday. From there the managers consulted with their own reports to choose another day of the week for workers from each separate unit to come in.

The managers also agreed on a company-wide "no meeting day" so that everyone could keep their heads down and work individually. They considered the effect that work in different time zones would have on their employees, too.

Of course, people who lived in a shoebox studio apartment or those who were overrun by roommates were welcome to come in and work whenever they pleased. But all employees, whatever their living situations and working preferences, had their touchstone days where they convened to get work done together.

A holistic manager is aware of workers' personal situations and tries to offer flexibility when possible. If it's a matter of their mental health, and they are suffering from serious depression, anxiety, or burnout, then work needs to take a backseat immediately as the employee takes a break and/or seeks out proper outside help. This is why managers need training in detecting and dealing with psychological issues.

When it comes to accommodating an employee's home life, managers will sometimes find themselves engaged in a balancing act. Yes, flexibility can be offered when possible. But at the same time, the work must get done—sometimes in person—and almost no one will be able to obtain the exact setup that they desire. There will always be some amount of give and take and compromise. If an employee can't take calls at 4:30 p.m. because he needs to pick up his child at day care, then his manager might need to call him at 8 p.m. to review an important presentation for the next day.

Suppose an employee must take care of an aging parent, or has two toddlers, or is dealing with a chronic illness. An ideal work situation for that person will probably differ from the setup for a single employee who lives alone (and who may actually prefer to come into the office most of the time).

An empathic manager will try to craft individual work-from-home arrangements that do not directly conflict with the company's goals. Again, this is something that a senior leader has neither the time nor the knowledge to accomplish. If done sensitively by the middle manager, the benefits it yields in employee satisfaction will be enormous.

Here, though, a potential problem rears its head: perceptions of unfairness. Imagine two workers who have similar jobs, both married, both with two children. One worker is told that she must come in three days a week, while the other is barely required to come in at all. The first worker begins seething with resentment over the perceived favoritism. She wouldn't mind spending more time with her kids at home too, after all. Her job satisfaction starts plummeting. Finally, she summons the nerve to talk to her manager about the situation. And then she learns her coworker has an elderly mother with dementia living with him, and is helping to care for her.

A concept known as process fairness can go a long way toward helping employees accept differences in their work arrangements.[12] And once again, the middle manager is the person best equipped to achieve it.

Process fairness includes three major steps: allowing employees to have genuine input in the decisions surrounding major changes; ensuring that changes are communicated clearly and with ample advance warning; and making sure that managers explain the rationale behind the changes while listening to and empathizing with workers' concerns.

If managers take those steps, employees are much more inclined to accept varying work-from-home arrangements. Even if they don't get what they want, as long as they feel they have been heard, they are more likely to accept a disruptive change.

It's a myth that managers need to treat all their employees equally. In reality, they need to treat their employees *equitably*. There's a big difference between the two, and one that the managers of the future will need to understand as they increasingly move the work to the people instead of the people to the work.

 **TAKEAWAYS**

Rethinking the Role of the Middle

The challenge: Too many workplaces are stuck in a headquarters model, both literally and figuratively, where leaders see employees as full-time equivalents who need to do the work wherever and however the organization sees fit. This ignores the importance of aligning each individual worker's purpose with corporate purpose as a way to improve productivity and engagement—and reduce attrition.

Why middle managers are key to meeting the challenge: Only middle managers can tailor the overall corporate purpose to the purpose of each team and its individual members. And only they can create customized hybrid work options that serve both the organization and its individual workers.

How senior leaders can help: Executives can make sure that middle managers have the time—and are rewarded for—matching employees to the work that best suits them, even if that means moving them to another department. Senior leaders must also loosen their grip on power and trust their middle managers to produce department-specific working arrangements that best serve their teams.

The Success of Managers Starts with Senior Leaders

Learning to Share the Power

Fred, the CEO of a fast-growing food-processing company, was sitting back in his office chair, just about to think through the next stages of his expansion strategy in Asia, when he was interrupted by the ping of an email. It was from his chief financial officer, and the subject line was: For you to approve.

Fred called up the email. His signature was required to replace the company credit card of one of the firm's line managers. After he signed the approval, Fred turned off his email notifications to ensure he wouldn't be interrupted again. It took him a few minutes to settle into deep-thinking mode. But then, just a few minutes after that, there was a harried knock at the door.

It was his assistant. "I'm sorry sir, but HR needs you to sign off on this hire," she said, showing him the employment contract for a new line worker. Fred scribbled his signature and then, after his assistant closed the door behind her, tried to get back to the Asia strategy. But by then, he simply couldn't concentrate, and so he spent the remaining hour before lunch answering emails and entering the names of his competitors into the Google search engine.

This is not an unrealistic story. We really have come across CEOs who, even as their companies grow into billion-dollar enterprises, insist on retaining control over the smallest of decisions. Some of them make a feeble attempt at spreading out decision rights to their managers, only to rescind them later because they are, after all, the ones who know best. This is incredibly demotivating for the managers sitting in the middle of this bait-and-switch.

Yes, Fred was an extreme micromanager. But to us his story is a metaphor for what most senior leaders do—even those who believe they are good at delegating. They fail to empower the people below them to do the work that they are uniquely suited to do. And their middle managers in particular have suffered the consequences.

The CEO's attitude can't help but replicate and reverberate throughout the organization, so that his middle managers, who would also like time to think and plan, are also robbed of the opportunity to do it.

I Don't Trust You

What is behind this way of operating? Basically, it comes down to a lack of trust. This is something we heard from a host of middle managers (who did not work for McKinsey clients) when we interviewed them individually.

These are some of the messages that middle managers are getting from their senior leaders:

- I don't trust you to make good business decisions, so I need you to synthesize the work below you and then present it to a person above you.

- I don't trust you to be able to find a way of getting more out of your people, so I want you to do some "real work" on the side.

- I don't trust you to make good travel decisions, so I need you to submit a travel form for approval.

Too many senior leaders are burdening managers with administrative duties that can be eliminated, automated, or assigned to other people. In effect, executives are prioritizing bureaucracy over trust.

Middle managers want authority, autonomy, and discretion. They want to provide input on strategy. They don't want to fill out forms. Yet filling out forms, following rules, and checking boxes has become a big part of their job. Not only that, when something goes wrong—as it often does—they are the ones blamed for following the rules that someone else created. On top of that, executives often expect their managers to perform individual contributor roles, too.

Some leaders have tried to put a positive spin on this practice by advocating a player-coach model of management. It sounds nice in theory: in a seamless progression, managers can both do the work at which they excel, and coach others to reach the same level. The problem is that both sides of the role become overloaded. And often, managers are not trained to be effective coaches, so they naturally gravitate toward the player or individual contributor role at the expense of the coach role. And when a manager is balancing two jobs instead of doing one, and they are poorly trained on top of that, guess what effect that has on their leadership abilities?

It is no wonder, then, that middle managers have such a bad reputation. And it is no wonder that this layer has often been seen—including by management consultants—as the simplest, least damaging, and most financially beneficial place to cut costs.

The problem, though, is not the job—it's what the job has become. Too many organizations equate middle management with bloated bureaucracy. But that's not the middle managers' fault. The blame for saddling managers with bureaucratic tasks rests squarely with senior leaders. And it's up to them to do something about it.

The answer is not to cut from the middle ranks. The answer is to transform the way the middle is perceived and (literally) how the middle works. This starts from the top, with executives loosening their grip on power and transferring more of it to the middle.

The first thing that needs to happen is a mindset shift. It's time that more senior leaders recognize that people are an organization's most important asset. And therefore the employees who recruit, hire, train, develop, and retain people—the middle managers—are the most important asset of all.

Too many executives are undercutting the value of their managers, and they're losing money in the process because too many employees are not being developed to their full potential. We have come across large organizations—with tens of thousands of employees and billions in revenue—that have seemingly forgotten to take care of and develop their middle managers. It's no wonder that managers don't know how to manage—they are essentially expected to learn via osmosis. This became especially acute during the pandemic, when the weight of supporting widely dispersed teams of individual contributors fell on managers, but often these same managers were not given any guidance on how to do it.

There is a satisfying parallel between how we are urging senior leaders to lead their managers and how we want the managers themselves to lead their own reports. New best practices will start from the top and flow throughout the organization. So, how can senior leaders get to a place where their middle managers are front and center? First, they need to answer two main questions:

- What do we want our middle managers to be doing? The answer could be some form of: We want them to serve as coaches, connectors, and navigators for the people who report to them, along with people throughout the organization.

- What are they doing right now? Chances are the answer is: Not very much of the above at all.

Our survey of middle managers showed that many feel they are spending time on low-value tasks like administration and individual contributor work, and not as much time on high-value work like coaching and developing their reports.[1] Senior leaders can make progress by becoming fully aware of the details behind this disconnect.

Then comes the hard part: making the changes that put middle managers first, and—at least for a while—prioritizing that effort above all else. A big part of this will involve thoughtfully deciding which tasks should and should not be part of the manager's role.

Even when they know they need to shake up their middle-management ranks, many senior leaders hate to hear this. Why? Mainly because of inertia and expediency. Here are some excuses: We've always done it this way. Change is hard. Rebundling and reassigning tasks takes time. Some projects may need to be delayed.

And when a manager is also good at a particular frontline job, it seems like a two-fer to have them do it one or two days a week. Who is going to do the extra work if those tasks are taken off their plate?

Time to Reassess Roles

There's another hard thing that senior leaders will need to face: Some of the people who are currently middle managers will need to be removed from those roles. That's because they never should have been hired or promoted to these positions in the first place. It's another practice from above that helped give the term "middle manager" a bad name.

In chapter 2, we told you about managers who settle into an organizational "permafrost," where they zealously guard the status quo and are quick to come up with reasons why every new idea is bad. In chapters 2 and 3, we told you about the practice of reflexively promoting excellent individual contributors because of an outdated mindset that the only way you can move up is to move into management. And in chapter 9 we told you about a tendency for cowardly managers to move underperforming employees to another department; in some cases this involves a promotion to an open middle-management spot where the employee has an opportunity to perform poorly in a brand-new way, this time bringing down their direct reports with them.

Obviously, in an organization that decides to put middle managers first, employees like these cannot stay where they are, so they will need to be redeployed. It should be fairly easy to find a new spot for individual contributors who were mistakenly moved to management, and to put them on a promotional career track within their area of expertise.

It's possible that some underperforming managers can be trained to be effective, or matched with a team that is a better fit. As for the rest, they will probably need to be thoughtfully transitioned out of the role. Eventually, people who are not suited to become middle managers become an organizational hazard.

At this point, though, senior leaders can't let this opportunity to permanently reduce head count tempt them. They must hire and promote for the now-open positions, and do so wisely. They can begin by identifying the most critical managerial roles in the organization—in other words, the ones that will generate the most profit and revenue in the future, and also the ones that will involve the highest risk (such as industries with major safety and data breach concerns). Then they can commit to putting the best managers in those critical roles. All middle managers matter, but put in this context, some matter more than others.

Understanding the Value of Managers

Most companies do a good job of putting a value on individual contributor and team leader roles. But provided that they are skilled,
trained, and empowered, middle managers have a reach that represents much more value than that of any single person below them. Yet
most leaders neglect to take steps to measure that value.

Once these high-value positions are pinpointed and filled, senior
leaders then can identify the most influential people in their organization. How to find these people? It can be done through a survey
with some form of a single question: "Who do you turn to when you
want to find out what's going on around here?" Inevitably, the same
names will turn up on many of the surveys.

Not all high-value managers are influencers. And not all influencers hold high-value roles. The key is to home in on what we call "the
critical few," who are both high-value and influential.[2] Senior leaders
will want to bring these managers into the tent with them to make
the most important strategic decisions. Beyond that, there are three
other categories of managers:

Microphones and megaphones: These are influencers who do not hold
high-value roles. They may not be among the critical few, but when these
people talk, other employees listen. They play a vital role that senior
leaders can nurture by deliberately feeding them information that will
find its way into conversations both small (microphones) and large
(megaphones). By striving to keep influencers informed and inspired,
and then letting them loose as communicators and translators, executives can help pump energy and excitement throughout the organization.

Value at risk: These managers are in high-value roles, but they have little
influence. Though smart and innovative, they may not be connected

enough to come up with good ideas in the first place. Or, if they do have good ideas, they lack the kind of reach that could bring them to fruition. Leaders need to give these high-value managers a push into the networks that can enable them to generate ideas and execute plans.

Waiting to be shaped and deployed: The remaining group of managers, though not in the top tier in terms of value or influence, can still make a difference if leaders are thoughtful about their skills and attributes. Placing them on high-value projects, or proactively connecting them with influencers, could be just the motivation they need to shine.

Once managers are hired, promoted, or transferred, the next step is for senior leaders to lavish time and money on training them to be the most effective people-leaders they can be. This can include a combination of classroom training and hands-on individual coaching, and it can follow a leadership development model that clearly articulates the organization's goals.

Executives can also change the way they evaluate their middle managers. Reward middle managers not just based on the revenue and profit that their departments produce; also reward them based on team performance, along with team health as measured by factors like attrition and engagement. The best managers are talent magnets (people want to work for them) and talent multipliers (help people shine brighter and achieve more than they ever thought possible). Senior leaders also need to be crystal clear about not just the outcomes but the behavior they want to see from their managers. Behaviors can include providing a supportive, uplifting, and inspiring environment. And also: not being a jerk.

We have come across managers who achieve great outcomes but are condescending bullies to their reports, while other managers are really fun and nice people but fail to achieve the desired results. Both outcomes *and* behavior need to be clarified and evaluated for a manager to be truly successful.

To transform their middle management ranks, senior leaders can also:

- Make sure the organization has a clearly defined statement of purpose, and that it is aligned with their managers' purpose.

- Do everything they can to keep their middle managers where they are, by promoting them within the role, and rewarding them the way executives are rewarded.

- Signal to employees that these are the most desirable positions in the organization. The message should be clear: This job is a destination, not a way station.

- Break up organizational silos by encouraging middle managers to meet regularly and share best practices.

- Sustain or create a culture of psychological safety where middle managers are not afraid to speak truth to power. In their unique position close to the ground, but not too close, they can be the first ones to detect serious systemic problems, and suggest ways to solve them.

- Show compassion for their managers, just as we have urged managers to show compassion for their own reports.

Remember, managers have some of the hardest jobs out there. Surveys show they are the most depressed and stressed category of worker because they're in charge of outcomes that they didn't necessarily plan or might not even agree with. Before getting down to business, ask them how they are, not as a formality but because you really want to know, on a personal and professional level. Hopefully, with a shift in mindset, some of the causes of that stress will ease. Recognize that middle managers cannot be truly effective unless you give them autonomy and flexibility. By removing the tasks that weigh them down, and empowering them to make their own decisions, you elevate their work and allow them to elevate the work of those who report to them.

A mindset of "learned helplessness" among managers seems to permeate many organizations, said the chief human resource officer at a large bank whom we interviewed. Her company employs more than one thousand bank managers, and there are big differences between the best bank managers and all the others, she says. The top managers have a sense of ownership of their branch. The best managers are also entrepreneurial, and the bank has encouraged them to think that way. In turn, "They create a sense of ownership among their employees to set higher goals and to see what's possible," she said. "The pride they feel as a collective team when they accomplish something is unbelievable."

Too many managers feel as if they're just a cog in the wheel and that they don't really matter. As a result, they underestimate the way they could transform their teams. What managers don't realize is that their sense of helplessness and cynicism is actually a form of negative energy that has a big impact.

It's clear to the human resource officer that whether it's positive or negative, middle managers have enormous influence—and that it can be used to either accelerate strategy and cultural change, or stop it in its tracks.

Share the Power

We see too many leaders who want to hoard power rather than release it to others. Like Fred, the CEO of the manufacturing company who needed to sign off on every decision, they view empowering others as a sign of weakness. But in fact, it is the opposite.

These executives are clinging to a twentieth-century view of leadership that puts shareholder value above all other values. Looking at their mandate through this lens, leaders tend to see their roles as

TABLE 10-1

The four modern roles of senior leaders

Visionary	Coach
• Communicates the organization's overarching purpose • Serves as a master storyteller • Listens and responds to insights and concerns across the company	• Makes sure managers receive adequate training • Serves as a personal coach to others • Encourages multiple viewpoints and experimentation
Architect	**Catalyst**
• Designs an open-ended rather than a top-down structure • Challenges assumptions and shifts resources to meet changing demands • Empowers managers to solve problems	• Removes obstacles that prevent progress • Improves connections between departments • Helps connect projects with the overall vision • Creates an atmosphere of wholeness and inclusivity

Source: McKinsey People & Organization Performance Practice.

planners (coming up with a strategy and turning it into a plan); directors (divvying up responsibility for the plan); and controllers (keeping a tight rein on everyone in charge of the plan so it doesn't diverge from the strategy).

But a twenty-first century view of leadership is much more expansive. It values not just shareholders but also employees, customers, suppliers, partners, and society as a whole. It requires sharing the power with managers, who in turn share the power with their employees. In this new view of leadership, we see executives replacing outmoded ways of operating with four new roles (table 10-1):[3]

Visionary: One of the most important things a senior leader can do is create and communicate the organization's vision and purpose. This serves as a North Star that can offer direction when the future is unclear and when it can be tempting to value short-term gain over long-term health. A visionary is an outstanding storyteller who can motivate employees—and especially managers—through specific and compelling narratives. Visionary leaders listen to and integrate the perspectives of others. They empower managers to tailor the vision for their teams so that it translates into positive outcomes.

Architect: From there, leaders then design an organization that is aligned with the vision. This is an extraordinarily complex task. Unlike the twentieth century, when the model was closed, top-down, and static, the new model is open, empowered, and ever-changing. It involves challenging previous assumption and shifting resources to meet evolving demands. A CEO and a few other top executives cannot possibly design all of this change. That is why as architects, they empower their managers and trust them to stay true to the overarching design.

Coach: Senior leaders can commit to training their managers in any skills they may lack, and to instill a culture of continuous learning. Training programs for managers are important, but they are not enough. Senior leaders must also serve as coaches themselves so that their managers can in turn become the best possible coaches. Executives can serve as role models, creating an environment in which multiple viewpoints are encouraged, experiments are welcome, and a certain amount of failure is expected. As coaches, they seek to inspire and motivate their managers to come up with solutions of their own, rather than issuing edicts from above.

Catalyst: As catalysts, senior leaders release energy that courses through the organization. They do this in four main ways:

- By removing obstacles that prevent teams from achieving their goals.

- By improving connections between different parts of the organizations.

- By helping departments and teams connect their projects with the organization's overall vision.

- By creating an atmosphere of wholeness and inclusivity, so that people feel free to bring their authentic selves to the workplace.

If executives can set aside the command-and-control style of leadership that no longer serves them, and embrace new roles as visionaries, architects, coaches, and catalysts, they will see the power they once hoarded released exponentially into the creative and capable hands of their managers.

A CEO Changes His Ways

It was the end of another long day—a day during which Fred had tried and failed yet again to work out his Asia expansion strategy. Wondering where the time had gone, he went over in his mind what he had actually done all day.

A lot of it, he realized, had involved approvals—budget approvals, hiring approvals, travel approvals. Another big part of it had involved receiving reassurances that his officers and managers were doing things the way they were supposed to be done—in short, his way.

Fred sat back in his chair and finally realized something: Even though his company now had a billion dollars in revenue, he was still running it as if he had to do everything. He had never truly let go of his one-person-show mindset. And there was a hidden assumption behind this mindset: that he couldn't trust anyone who worked for him to perform as well as he could.

It was Fred's aha moment. Because what did it say about his business acumen if he couldn't even trust the people he had chosen to hire?

But here's the thing: Fred had (mostly) chosen good people. He just hadn't given them the autonomy they needed to prove that they *could* be trusted.

And that's when things started to change at the manufacturing firm. Fred made a thorough list of all the things he wanted his managers to do, and, importantly, all the things he wanted them to stop doing.

Then he held a meeting with all the managers and officers of the firm. When he spoke, he was honest and showed vulnerability. He talked about the thrills and uncertainties of starting his own company twenty years earlier, and how through hard work and entrepreneurial thinking he had developed a new kind of food processing equipment that was much more efficient and safer than the ones that had come before it—so much so that the company had now grown to one thousand employees and $1 billion in revenue.

"I could never have reached this level of success without you," he told his managers. "But I'm not treating you that way, am I?"

The managers knew exactly what he was talking about. They couldn't help nodding (ever so slightly, out of politeness) in agreement.

But that was going to change starting now, Fred said. He talked about the company's expansion goals in Asia, and how its food-processing equipment could be a game changer in reducing world hunger.

"Keeping you under my thumb is wasting your talents and holding back the company's potential, and it's stopped us from getting our equipment to people who could benefit from it," he said. From now on, he told his managers, he would be taking steps to empower them.

And Fred was as good as his word—although his leadership journey was littered with pitfalls. At first he thought he could simply say to his managers, "Go forth and be empowered." But after a few months of this, some of his managers were still coming to him for approvals even though he had told them (once) that he now trusted them to handle those things on their own. And some of the newly empowered managers made such boneheaded decisions that he was sorely tempted to take back total control again.

At that point Fred realized a few of his managers were simply not cut out to be managers. So he moved most of those to individual contributor roles, while a few others resigned or, regrettably, had to be let go. But overall, Fred had chosen his managers well and placed them in positions where they were poised to excel. So what was missing? Management training, of course. Accustomed to pushing paper for years, these managers needed to develop new muscles.

So Fred temporarily put aside his expansion plans so he could devote most of his resources—both money and time—to manager training. It included comprehensive classroom training, but more importantly it also included individual hands-on coaching from Fred and his senior leadership team. The coaching occurred alongside the cadence of the work. The biggest projects—and the most urgent turning points in those projects—received the most hands-on guidance from above.

For six months, the training and coaching were going well—or at least they seemed to Fred to be going well. But then one day he asked himself: How do I really *know* things are going well? That they're actually moving the needle? And that's when he and his reports came up with a leadership development model designed to assess his managers' behavior and performance, and to hold them accountable for results.

Fred took the time to analyze: What kinds of qualities do my best managers exhibit? These included the ability to innovate, collaborate between departments, and to inspire reports. He arranged for an upward feedback survey to be given twice a year so that his managers could be evaluated on how well they had demonstrated those qualities.

He also came up with a performance scorecard that measured traditional metrics such as a team's revenue, profit margin, budgets and expenditures, and factors such as:

- Team performance

- Diversity of the team

- Attrition rate

- Open position rate

- Number of one-on-one conversations with reports

- Succession planning (who on your team could take your place)

- Employee engagement

Fred made sure to explain why all the elements of the scorecard were important, so that his managers understood them in the larger context of the company's purpose and goals. When there was a performance issue, an executive and a manager could consult the scorecard and discuss what was getting in the way of success. As with most performance issues, it was generally a skill-versus-will situation. And these could generally be resolved through one-on-one conversations.

One Year Later

A year later, Fred was sitting in his office. His email notifications were turned off, and he had told his assistant not to interrupt him for the rest of the morning. For the next two hours, he carefully thought through the next phase of his expansion strategy in Asia. In the past, he had never had time for deep thought like this.

Then Fred prepared to communicate the next steps of that strategy to his managers. He was fully confident that they could handle the challenge without him having to know about every detail. And that made him feel good.

Fred knew that because of the trust he had placed in his managers, his company was now well on its way to even greater success. It had taken him twenty years to figure it out, but he had finally learned that the talent of management is the management of talent.

It comes down to this: In shifting from a twentieth-century to a twenty-first-century model, senior leaders will need to reorient their perspective so that their own personal success is achieved by making sure the people below them are successful, too.

As a senior leader, think of the impact you can have—and the legacy you can leave—by growing the next two or three generations of leaders. Then, after a few of your middle managers do rise to the very topmost level, you will know that you have left your organization in the best of hands.

● TAKEAWAYS

Rethinking the Role of the Middle

The challenge: Middle managers have been reduced to a state of "learned helplessness" by executives who refuse to share their power and who waste their managerial talent on tasks that don't add the most value.

What senior leaders can do to meet the challenge: Executives can work to actually measure the value of their managers, and then train, coach, and inspire them to reach their full potential.

NOTES

Introduction

1. Bryan Hancock and Bill Schaninger, "Grief, Loss, Burnout: Navigating a New Emotional Landscape at Work," *McKinsey Organization Blog*, April 19, 2021, https://www.mckinsey.com/business-functions/people-and-organizational-performance/our-insights/the-organization-blog/grief-loss-burnout-navigating-a-new-emotional-landscape-at-work.

2. "Middle Manager Research Insights," McKinsey, May 2022. The online survey was conducted in the field with McKinsey's proprietary survey panel from March 29, 2022, to April 8, 2022, and garnered responses from 719 participants representing a range of regions, industries, company sizes, and functional specialties. The survey defined a middle manager as "a manager of one or more people who manage employees," and it screened out C-suite executives and respondents who had been in their current role—or in a similar management role—at their organization for less than six months. There were 258 respondents in the United States.

Chapter 1

1. Renee, Gavin, Larry, and Cora are middle managers who were interviewed by phone. A few identifying details, including their first names, have been changed to protect their anonymity. They are not McKinsey clients.

2. "Middle Manager Research Insights," McKinsey, May 2022.

3. "Middle Manager Research Insights."

4. "Anxious? Depressed? Blame It on Your Middle-Management Position," *Public Health Now*, Columbia University Mailman School of Public Health, August 19, 2015, https://www.publichealth.columbia.edu/public-health-now/news/anxious-depressed-blame-it-your-middle-management-position.

5. Erich M. Anicich and Jacob B. Hirsh, "Why Being a Middle Manager Is So Exhausting," *Harvard Business Review*, March 22, 2017, https://hbr.org/2017/03/why-being-a-middle-manager-is-so-exhausting.

6. "State of the American Manager: Analytics and Advice for Leaders," Gallup report, 2015, https://www.gallup.com/services/182138/state-american-manager.aspx.

7. Bonnie Dowling, Marino Mugayar-Baldocchi, Bill Schaninger, and Joachim Talloen, "The Brave New (Business) World," *McKinsey Organization Blog*, February 7, 2022, https://www.mckinsey.com/capabilities/people-and-organizational-performance/our-insights/the-organization-blog/the-brave-new-business-world.

8. McKinsey People and Organizational Performance analysis.

9. Bureau of Labor Statistics news release, November 4, 2022, https://www.bls.gov/news.release/pdf/empsit.pdf.

10. Aaron De Smet, Bonnie Dowling, Bryan Hancock, and Bill Schaninger, "The Great Attrition is Making Hiring Harder. Are You Searching the Right Talent Pools?" *McKinsey Quarterly*, July 13, 2022, https://www.mckinsey.com/capabilities/people-and-organizational-performance/our-insights/the-great-attrition-is-making-hiring-harder-are-you-searching-the-right-talent-pools.

11. Aaron De Smet, Bonnie Dowling, Marino Mugayar-Baldocchi, and Bill Schaninger, "'Great Attrition' or 'Great Attraction'? The Choice is Yours," *McKinsey Quarterly*, September 8, 2021, https://www.mckinsey.com/business-functions/people-and-organizational-performance/our-insights/great-attrition-or-great-attraction-the-choice-is-yours.

12. McKinsey People and Organizational Performance analysis.

13. McKinsey retail industry analysis.

Chapter 2

1. William H. Whyte, *The Organization Man* (New York: Simon & Schuster, 1956).

2. Jonas Hjort, Hannes Malmberg, and Todd Schoellman, "The Missing Middle Managers: Labor Costs, Firm Structure, and Development," National Bureau of Economic Research, October 2022, https://www.nber.org/papers/w30592.

3. Steven F. Dichter, "The Organization of the 90's," *McKinsey Quarterly*, March 1, 1992.

4. James A Champy and Michael Martin Hammer, *Reengineering the Corporation: A Manifesto for Business Revolution* (Collins Business Essentials, 1993).

5. See, respectively, E. G. Chambers, Mark Foulon, Helen Handfield-Jones, and Steven M. Hankin, "The War for Talent," *McKinsey Quarterly*, January 1998, 44–57; and Ed Michaels, Helen Handfield-Jones, and Beth Axelrod, *The War for Talent* (Boston: Harvard Business School Press, 2001).

6. Susann Gjerde and Mats Alvesson, "Sandwiched: Exploring Role and Identity of Middle Managers in the Genuine Middle," *Human Relations* 73, no. 1 (2020): 124–51, https://journals.sagepub.com/doi/10.1177/0018726718823243.

7. Christopher J. Goodman and Steven M. Mance, "Employment Loss and the 2007–09 Recession: An Overview," *Monthly Labor Review*, Bureau of Labor Statistics, April 2011.

8. Christian Camerota, "The Unintended Effects of Open Office Space," *Harvard Business School News*, July 9, 2018, https://www.hbs.edu/news/articles/Pages/bernstein-open-offices.aspx.

9. *Office Space*, directed by Mike Judge (20th Century Fox, 1999), 89 minutes.

10. Aaron De Smet, Bonnie Dowling, Marino Mugayar-Baldocchi, and Bill Schaninger, "'Great Attrition' or 'Great Attraction'? The Choice is Yours," *McKinsey Quarterly*, September 8, 2021, https://www.mckinsey.com/business-functions/people-and-organizational-performance/our-insights/great-attrition-or-great-attraction-the-choice-is-yours.

11. "Executives Feel the Strain of Leading in the 'New Normal,'" Future Forum Pulse, October 2022, https://futureforum.com/research/pulse-report-fall-2022-executives-feel-strain-leading-in-new-normal/.

12. Jo Constantz, "The Middle Managers Are Not Alright," Bloomberg website, October 20, 2022, https://www.bloomberg.com/news/articles/2022-10-20/middle -managers-most-at-risk-of-burnout-in-return-to-office-era.

Chapter 3

1. Kelsey, who is not a McKinsey client, was interviewed by phone. Her name and some details have been changed to protect her identity.

2. Theodore Ross, "Meet the Short Order Cooks So Good Waffle House Officially Calls Them Rockstars," *Medium*, January 9, 2019, https://medium.com/s/story/meet -the-short-order-cooks-so-fucking-good-waffle-house-officially-calls-them-rockstars -caf47c31912.

3. Vijay Govindarajan, Nikhil Sikka, and Anup Srivastava, "The Uncertainty of Middle Management Jobs—and How to Stay Relevant," *California Management Review*, Fall 2022.

4. "Middle Manager Research Insights," McKinsey, May 2022.

5. Aaron de Smet, Bonnie Dowling, Bryan Hancock, and Bill Schaninger, "The Great Attrition Is Making Hiring Harder. Are You Searching the Right Talent Pools?" *McKinsey Quarterly*, July 13, 2022, https://www.mckinsey.com/business-functions /people-and-organizational-performance/our-insights/the-great-attrition-is-making -hiring-harder-are-you-searching-the-right-talent-pools.

Chapter 4

1. Russell Redman, "Amazon Unveils First Amazon Fresh Grocery Store in Wood- land Hills," *Supermarket News*, August 27, 2020, https://www.supermarketnews.com /retail-financial/amazon-unveils-first-amazon-fresh-grocery-store-woodland-hills.

2. Nicole Dusanek, "How Culture and Creativity Saved Thousands of Delta Jobs," Delta News Hub, September 15, 2020, https://news.delta.com/how-culture-and -creativity-saved-thousands-delta-jobs.

3. Sara Brown, "The Lure of 'So-So Technology' and How to Avoid It," *Ideas Made to Matter*, MIT Management Sloan School, October 31, 2019, https://mitsloan.mit.edu /ideas-made-to-matter/lure-so-so-technology-and-how-to-avoid-it.

4. "What Is a Walmart Academy? How They're Building Confidence and Careers," Walmart website, April 17, 2017, https://corporate.walmart.com/newsroom /opportunity/20170417/what-is-a-walmart-academy-how-theyre-building-confidence -and-careers.

5. "Live Better U Fact Sheet," updated July 26, 2021, Walmart website, https:// corporate.walmart.com/media-library/document/live-better-u-fact-sheet-july-2021 /_proxyDocument?id=0000017a-e56b-d458-ab7f-f7ebc2ee0000.

6. "Wholesale Upskilling: Walmart's Workforce Value Proposition," *Managing the Future of Work* podcast, Harvard Business School, May 26, 2022, https://www.hbs.edu /managing-the-future-of-work/podcast/Pages/podcast-details.aspx?episode=23233211.

7. Amy Goldfinger and Lorraine Stomski, "At Walmart, There Is a Path for Every- one," Walmart website, May 15, 2022, https://corporate.walmart.com/newsroom/2022 /05/15/at-walmart-there-is-a-path-for-everyone.

8. Jacques Bughin, Eric Hazan, Susan Lund, Peter Dahlstrom, Anna Wiesinger, and Amrash Subramaniam, "Skill Shift: Automation and the Future of the Workforce,"

McKinsey Discussion Paper, May 23, 2018, https://www.mckinsey.com/featured
-insights/future-of-work/skill-shift-automation-and-the-future-of-the-workforce.

9. Steve Lohr, "Economists Pin More Blame on Tech for Rising Inequality," *New York Times*, January 11, 2022, https://www.nytimes.com/2022/01/11/technology
/income-inequality-technology.html.

10. "Gartner Predicts 69 percent of Routine Work Currently Done by Managers Will Be Fully Automated by 2024," Gartner website, January 23, 2020, https://www.gartner
.com/en/newsroom/press-releases/2020-01-23-gartner-predicts-69--of-routine-work
-currently-done-b.

11. Naina Dhingra, Andrew Amo, Bill Schaninger, and Matt Schrimper, "Help Your Employees Find Purpose—or Watch Them Leave," McKinsey website, April 5,
2021. https://www.mckinsey.com/business-functions/people-and-organizational
-performance/our-insights/help-your-employees-find-purpose-or-watch-them-leave.

Chapter 5

1. Greg Iacurci, "The Great Resignation Continues, as 44% of Workers Look for a New Job," CNBC website, March 22, 2022, https://www.cnbc.com/2022/03/22/great
-resignation-continues-as-44percent-of-workers-seek-a-new-job.html.

2. Aaron De Smet, Bonnie Dowling, Marino Mugayar-Baldocchi, and Bill Schaninger, "'Great Attrition' or 'Great Attraction?' The Choice is Yours," *McKinsey Quarterly*, September 8, 2021, https://www.mckinsey.com/business-functions/people-and
-organizational-performance/our-insights/great-attrition-or-great-attraction-the
-choice-is-yours.

3. "Why the Onboarding Experience Is Key for Retention," *Gallup Blog*, April 11,
2018, https://www.gallup.com/workplace/235121/why-onboarding-experience-key
-retention.aspx.

4. Talya N. Bauer, "Onboarding New Employees: Maximizing Success," SHRM Foundation's Effective Practice Guidelines Series, 2010, https://www.shrm.org
/foundation/ourwork/initiatives/resources-from-past-initiatives/documents
/onboarding%20new%20employees.pdf.

5. Emily Wetherell and Bailey Nelson, "8 Practical Tips for a Better Onboarding Process," *Gallup Workplace Blog*, August 12, 2021, https://www.gallup.com/workplace
/353096/practical-tips-leaders-better-onboarding-process.aspx.

6. "The Essentials: Retaining Talent," *Women at Work* podcast, *Harvard Business Review*, April 4, 2022, https://hbr.org/podcast/2022/04/the-essentials-retaining
-talent.

7. "The 5 Languages of Appreciation in the Workplace," Appreciation at Work website, https://www.appreciationatwork.com/5-languages-appreciation-workplace
-improve-employee-engagement/.

8. Naina Dhingra, Andrew Samo, Bill Schaninger, and Matt Schrimper, "Help Your Employees Find Purpose—or Watch Them Leave," McKinsey website, April 5,
2021, https://www.mckinsey.com/business-functions/people-and-organizational
-performance/our-insights/help-your-employees-find-purpose-or-watch-them-leave.

9. Aaron De Smet, Bonnie Dowling, Marino Mugayar-Baldocchi, and Bill Schaninger, "'Great Attrition' or 'Great Attraction?' The Choice is Yours," *McKinsey Quarterly*, September 8, 2021, https://www.mckinsey.com/business-functions/people-and
-organizational-performance/our-insights/great-attrition-or-great-attraction-the
-choice-is-yours.

Chapter 6

1. Jude King, "How Great Leaders Communicate Big Vision So That Others Want to Join In," *Medium*, November 29, 2019, https://medium.com/@Jude.M/how-great -leaders-communicate-big-vision-so-that-others-want-to-join-in-d3296e7ca37e.

2. "Becoming a Cast Member at Disney Parks," Disney Careers website, https:// parksjobs.disneycareers.com/application-process.

3. Bryan Hancock and Bill Schaninger, "Quiet Quitting and Performance Management," *McKinsey Talks Talent* podcast, October 26, 2022.

4. "Psychological Safety and the Critical Role of Leadership Development," McKinsey survey, February 11, 2021, https://www.mckinsey.com/business-functions/people -and-organizational-performance/our-insights/psychological-safety-and-the-critical -role-of-leadership-development.

5. Amy Edmondson, *The Fearless Organization: Cultivating Psychological Safety in the Workplace for Learning, Innovation, and Growth* (Hoboken, NJ: Wiley, 2018).

6. Bill Schaninger and Taylor Lauricella, "The Questions You Ask Drive the Action You See," *McKinsey Organization Blog*, April 14, 2020, https://www.mckinsey.com /capabilities/people-and-organizational-performance/our-insights/the-organization -blog/the-questions-you-ask-drive-the-action-you-see.

7. Taiichi Ohno, "Ask 'Why' Five Times About Every Matter," Toyota website, March 2006, https://www.toyota-myanmar.com/about-toyota/toyota-traditions /quality/ask-why-five-times-about-every-matter.

8. Daniel Goleman and Richard E. Boyatzis, "Emotional Intelligence Has 12 Elements. Which Do You Need to Work On?" *Harvard Business Review*, February 6, 2017, https://hbr.org/2017/02/emotional-intelligence-has-12-elements-which-do-you-need -to-work-on.

9. Bryan Hancock and Bill Schaninger, "Grief, Loss, Burnout: Navigating a New Emotional Landscape at Work," *McKinsey Organization Blog*, April 19, 2021, https:// www.mckinsey.com/business-functions/people-and-organizational-performance /our-insights/the-organization-blog/grief-loss-burnout-navigating-a-new-emotional -landscape-at-work.

10. Heidi K. Gardner and Mark Mortensen, "Managers are Trapped in a Performance-Compassion Dilemma," *Harvard Business Review*, April 7, 2022, https:// hbr.org/2022/04/managers-are-trapped-in-a-performance-compassion-dilemma.

11. David Rock, "Stop Telling Managers to Be Empathetic. Try This Instead," *Fast Company*, November 11, 2021, https://www.fastcompany.com/90695010/stop-telling -managers-to-be-empathetic-try-this-instead.

Chapter 7

1. Aaron De Smet, Bonnie Dowling, Marino Mugayar-Baldocchi, and Bill Schaninger, "'Great Attrition' or 'Great Attraction?' The Choice is Yours," *McKinsey Quarterly*, September 8, 2021, https://www.mckinsey.com/business-functions/people-and -organizational-performance/our-insights/great-attrition-or-great-attraction-the -choice-is-yours.

2. Scott Judd, Eric O'Rourke, and Adam Grant, "Employee Surveys Are Still One of the Best Ways to Measure Engagement," *Harvard Business Review*, March 14, 2018, https://hbr.org/2018/03/employee-surveys-are-still-one-of-the-best-ways-to-measure -engagement.

3. "The Essentials: Retaining Talent," *Women at Work* podcast, *Harvard Business Review*, April 4, 2022, https://hbr.org/podcast/2022/04/the-essentials-retaining-talent.

4. Alexander DiLeonardo, Taylor Lauricella, and Bill Schaninger, "Survey Fatigue? Blame the Leader, Not the Question," *McKinsey Organization Blog*, May 10, 2021, https://www.mckinsey.com/business-functions/people-and-organizational-performance/our-insights/the-organization-blog/survey-fatigue-blame-the-leader-not-the-question.

5. Joseph B. Fuller, Manjari Raman, Eva Sage-Gavin, and Kristin Hines, September 2021, "Hidden Workers: Untapped Talent," Harvard Business School Project on Managing the Future of Work and Accenture.

6. Zahira Jaser, Dimitra Patrakaki, Rachel Starr, and Ernesto Oyabide-Magana, "Where Automated Job Interviews Fall Short," *Harvard Business Review*, January 27, 2022, https://hbr.org/2022/01/where-automated-job-interviews-fall-short.

7. *Occupational Outlook Handbook*, Bureau of Labor Statistics. September 8, 2022.

8. Jit Kee Chin, Mikael Hagstroem, Ari Labrikian, and Khaled Rifai, "Advanced Analytics: Nine Insights From the C-Suite," McKinsey website, July 5, 2017, https://www.mckinsey.com/business-functions/quantumblack/our-insights/advanced-analytics-nine-insights-from-the-c-suite.

9. Scott Berinato, "Data Science and the Art of Persuasion," *Harvard Business Review Magazine*, January–February 2019, https://hbr.org/2019/01/data-science-and-the-art-of-persuasion.

10. Solly Brown, Darshit Gandhi, Louise Herring, and Ankur Puri, "The Analytics Academy: Bridging the Gap Between Human and Artificial Intelligence," *McKinsey Quarterly*, September 25, 2019, https://www.mckinsey.com/business-functions/quantumblack/our-insights/the-analytics-academy-bridging-the-gap-between-human-and-artificial-intelligence.

11. Tobias Baer and Vishnu Kamalnath, "Addressing Bias in Machine Learning Problem Solving," McKinsey website, November 10, 2017, https://www.mckinsey.com/business-functions/risk-and-resilience/our-insights/controlling-machine-learning-algorithms-and-their-biases.

Chapter 8

1. Steve Lohr, "Millions Have Lost a Step Into the Middle Class, Researchers Say," *New York Times*, January 14, 2022, https://www.nytimes.com/2022/01/14/business/middle-class-jobs-study.html.

2. Ram Charan, Dominic Barton, and Dennis Cary, *Talent Wins* (Boston: Harvard Business Review Press, 2018).

Chapter 9

1. Aaron De Smet, Bonnie Dowling, Marino Mugayar-Baldocchi, and Bill Schaninger, "'Great Attrition' or 'Great Attraction?' The Choice is Yours," *McKinsey Quarterly*, September 8, 2021, https://www.mckinsey.com/business-functions/people-and-organizational-performance/our-insights/great-attrition-or-great-attraction-the-choice-is-yours.

2. Naina Dhingra, Andrew Samo, Bill Schaninger, and Matt Schrimper, "Help Your Employees Find Purpose—or Watch Them Leave," McKinsey website, April 5,

2021, https://www.mckinsey.com/business-functions/people-and-organizational
-performance/our-insights/help-your-employees-find-purpose-or-watch-them-leave.

3. Micah Solomon, "Ritz-Carlton President Herve Humler's Leadership, Culture, and Customer Service Secrets," *Forbes*, April 21, 2015, https://www.forbes.com/sites /micahsolomon/2015/04/21/ritz-carlton-president-herve-humlers-leadership-culture -and-customer-service-secrets/?sh=405606483b55.

4. Micah Solomon, "How to Bring Ritz-Carlton Caliber Customer Service to Any Type of Business," *Forbes*, February 23, 2020, https://www.forbes.com/sites /micahsolomon/2020/02/23/how-to-bring-ritz-carlton-caliber-customer-service-to -any-type-of-business/?sh=5a89175657dd.

5. "What's Your (Corporate Purpose) Sweet Spot?" McKinsey Featured Insights, January 6, 2021, https://www.mckinsey.com/featured-insights/coronavirus-leading -through-the-crisis/charting-the-path-to-the-next-normal/whats-your-corporate -purpose-sweet-spot.

6. Dhingra et al., "Help Your Employees."

7. James C. Collins and Jerry I. Porras, "Building Your Company's Vision," *Harvard Business Review*, September 1, 1996.

8. Zoe Schiffer, "Apple Employees Push Back Against Returning to the Office in Internal Letter," *The Verge*, June 4, 2021, https://www.theverge.com/2021/6/4/22491629 /apple-employees-push-back-return-office-internal-letter-tim-cook.

9. Susan Lund, Anu Madgavkar, James Manyika, and Sven Smit, "What's Next for Remote Work: An Analysis of 2,000 Tasks, 800 Jobs, and Nine Counties," McKinsey Featured Insights, November 23, 2020, https://www.mckinsey.com/featured-insights /future-of-work/whats-next-for-remote-work-an-analysis-of-2000-tasks-800-jobs -and-nine-countries.

10. Annamarie Mann, "Why We Need Best Friends at Work," *Gallup Workplace Blog*, January 15, 2018, https://www.gallup.com/workplace/236213/why-need-best-friends -work.aspx.

11. Catherine Fisher, "LinkedIn Study Reveals Work BFF's Make Us Happier at the Office," *LinkedIn Official Blog*, July 8, 2014, https://blog.linkedin.com/2014/07/08 /work-bffs.

12. Joel Brockner, "Why It's So Hard to Be Fair," *Harvard Business Review Magazine*, March 2006, https://hbr.org/2006/03/why-its-so-hard-to-be-fair.

Conclusion

1. "Middle Manager Research Insights," McKinsey, May 2022.

2. Bill Schaninger and Taylor Lauricella, "A Data-Backed Approach to Stakeholder Engagement," McKinsey Insights, May 28, 2020, https://www.mckinsey.com/business -functions/people-and-organizational-performance/our-insights/the-organization -blog/a-data-backed-approach-to-stakeholder-engagement.

3. Michael Lurie and Laura Tegelberg, "The New Roles of Leaders in 21st Century Organizations," *McKinsey Organization Blog*, September 23, 2019, https://www.mckinsey .com/business-functions/people-and-organizational-performance/our-insights/the -organization-blog/the-new-roles-of-leaders-in-21st-century-organizations.

INDEX

ACKNOWLEDGMENTS

Thank you to our McKinsey colleagues who are the real heroes who brought this book to life along with us. There are too many to count, though we'd like to specifically acknowledge a few steadfast team members without whom this book would not exist, including Marino Mugayar-Baldocchi, for managing the research process end-to-end and making sure we stayed on track; Heather Hanselman, for leading the manager survey fielding and analysis; Anne Blackman, for her support in the early days when the book was a mere idea and who helped bring the proposal to life; Raju Narisetti, the head of McKinsey Publishing; and Jacquie Hudson, for communications support. Thank you also to Lucia Rahilly and Laurel Moglen of the *McKinsey Talks Talent* podcast, which inspired many of the ideas within this book.

This book was written late at night and on weekends, and we put pen to paper on many a cross-country flight while simultaneously servicing clients. We recognize that corralling three spirited authors is no easy feat. We owe immense gratitude to Phyllis Korkki for supporting us in bringing our vision to fruition, learning with us, and tapping into our strengths so expertly.

Thank you to our editor, Jeff Kehoe at Harvard Business Review Press, for constructive feedback and constant check-ins along the way. We're also grateful to the entire editorial team at HBR Press. We specifically chose HBR Press because of their commitment to feedback throughout the process, and their collaboration yielded a better book.

Thank you to Lynn Johnston, our literary agent, for helping us find our voice and pushing us to make sure we were meeting the needs of our readers.

Thank you to Christine Collister, whose engaging graphic designs helped illustrate key ideas in the book.

We are grateful to our clients who have let us into their companies to both observe and build their manager capabilities. Throughout the course of writing the book, conversations with our clients about the importance of middle management kept us convinced that this book fills a great need. Client service is our mission, and we feel privileged to be able to serve our clients, many of whom inspired the stories within this book.

And thank you to our own managers throughout the years, too many to name, who have inspired us and helped us craft our own management philosophies.

And last but not least, we want to thank you, our readers, for reading this book. Whether you are a middle manager, lead middle managers, or aspire to one day become a middle manager, we hope at least a few of the nuggets in the book stay with you. We look forward to continuing to build middle managers' capabilities, because we believe deeply that the future of work rests in their hands. To that end, we would be grateful to continue the conversation, and we'd welcome feedback and insights. You can reach us at bill_schaninger@mckinsey.com, bryan _hancock@mckinsey.com, and emily_field@mckinsey.com.

Bill's acknowledgments—I would especially like to thank my partner, Becky, for her contributions to understanding the role of middle managers in for-profit and not-for-profit settings. I would also like to acknowledge Anna and Vaughn for their willingness to listen to previous episodes of *McKinsey Talks Talent* (this involved multiple instances of listening to the same episode and hearing me ask the same question: "How did I sound?"). Their collective tolerance and occasional quip about something being boring provided useful feedback (as only teenagers can).

I would also like to thank my son Will, who is at the beginning of his professional services career but has been listening to my musings about "just needing to run the place better." Initially Will just listened, and then he fully participated in the conversations that form my thinking.

Bryan's acknowledgments—I would like to thank my wife, Maryanne, for her support, inspiration, insights, and validation of the critical role managers have in shaping both business outcomes and how people feel about their time at work.

I would also like to thank my sons, Will and Hugh, for their interest in our work on managers, from listening to our podcasts and following our tweets, to seeing the applications of our work in their own lives.

Emily's acknowledgments—I would like to thank my husband, Ben MacWilliams, for his constant support, for being my steadfast cheerleader, and for sharing his own manager stories throughout the book-writing process. Thank you to my entire family for their encouragement.

ABOUT THE AUTHORS

BILL SCHANINGER grew up in a working-class family in Allentown, Pennsylvania, where his father was a printer and his mother was a bookkeeper. While in college he was a bouncer, which taught him how to change people's behavior quickly. He learned the same skill when, while still in school, he supervised a residential treatment unit for juvenile offenders. This was a middle management job, and he soon discovered how difficult it was to straddle the line of advancing his employer's agenda while also advocating for his team.

Bill came to understand that as a middle manager he had huge responsibilities without a great deal of control, and that he was frequently forced to sell an idea that wouldn't have been his own choice. He was struck by how tenuous the role of manager really is, because it depends on workers subordinating their own interests for a greater goal. Without that buy-in, the whole management structure falls apart.

After getting a PhD in management from Auburn University, Bill joined McKinsey, where he is now a senior partner. On the way, he served in middle management roles, for example while devising the company's Organizational Health Index. In some ways, he misses the hands-on work of middle management, of having a "baby" to call his own.

In his current role, Bill advises CEOs, government ministers, and senior executives on organizational health and improvement. Beyond client service, Bill continues to write, speak, and champion leading-edge thinking on organizational performance, change management, and all things talent.

BRYAN HANCOCK's first real job was as a bag boy at a Kroger grocery store outside Atlanta, and to this day it influences how he views working life and management. He'll never forget helping someone buy groceries using food stamps for the first time and not fully understanding the rules. Or hauling bags to customers' car trunks in 100-degree weather and noticing that the people with the fanciest cars tended not to tip. Or the butcher, noticing that Bryan was a hard worker, asking if he would like to be his assistant, with the understanding that this could lead to a steady upward career path at the company.

After graduating from Harvard Law School, Bryan joined the airline practice at McKinsey. That was in August 2001, and a month later came 9/11. Soon he was deep into problem-solving mode as travel demand plummeted. Bryan and others in the airline practice had to think of flexible ways to view scheduling and deploy labor amid a radically reduced demand for air travel. Quickly Bryan understood that middle managers were key to understanding both the details and the bigger picture in this very complicated puzzle.

Gradually, Bryan segued out of the airline practice and spent more time in the retail industry. While helping a retail chain understand why it had developed a mixed reputation as an employer, he met with senior leaders who prided themselves on how they were treating their workers and managers. In concrete measures such as salary and benefits, this company was actually ahead of many competitors.

So why the disconnect? After doing research on individual stores, Bryan and his team found a lack of consistency among store managers. In the stores with good managers, employees were happy. But complaints from employees with poor managers spread to the media and beyond, and rapid company growth was increasing the number of undertrained managers. The answer was to provide more consistent store-level training processes to help newer managers, and to improve the training and development of a managers and assistant managers.

Bryan, a leader of McKinsey's talent work, has also done research on the educational achievement gap because of its profound effect on the future workforce. While investigating why some schools perform better than others, he found that the biggest differences occurred not from state to state or from district to district, but among individual schools. And what tended to make individual schools excel? The effectiveness of their principals. People don't tend to think of principals as middle managers, but in fact they are the consummate middle managers, serving as crucial touchpoints between district administrators and rank-and-file teachers.

Bryan's experience with store managers and school principals has led him to realize that a company can have the smartest and most well-meaning CEO, and the most brilliant strategy, and yet whether it thrives really comes down to how that strategy is executed by its middle managers.

EMILY FIELD's personal mission, as far back as she can remember, has been to help others. In college, she interned at a nonprofit that helped low-income, high-potential students attain a high-quality education. From there, she knew she wanted to pursue a management consulting career as a way to help both individuals and organizations.

She gained a deep understand of the importance of managers in her first job out of college, when she was tasked with designing and implementing the post 9/11 strategy of a national law enforcement agency. The agency believed that developing its manager workforce was critical to protecting the country—so Emily set out to rebuild its leadership program across every managerial rank. It was in this role that she first realized that middle managers, who are so often neglected and forgotten, are actually a force multiplier that can transform an entire organization.

In her role at McKinsey, Emily is herself a middle manager who serves as a navigator and a coach. She must lead teams while also reporting to senior leaders. Her job is to provide clarity, solve problems, and get things done. She is accountable for making sure that team members meet or exceed expectations, while helping them realize their goals and have a fulfilling experience. In this way, she understands that middle managers need the time and the autonomy to think critically about problems and come up with their own solutions.

Emily's mission to help people came to the fore during the pandemic. She admits that she felt helpless when the pandemic began. Watching hardworking individuals lose their livelihoods while concerned about their health and safety made Emily think: "How can I help?" And she realized that other McKinsey consultants were asking the same question: What could they do at a time when some industries were suffering from a calamitous drop-off in business while others were experiencing unprecedented demand?

The answer was a talent exchange, where with the help of a tech company Emily and her team developed an algorithm that matched people who were on furlough with jobs that desperately needed to be filled. In this way, a furloughed hotel employee with good customer service and multitasking skills could be placed with a hospital that needed exactly those skills.

As the exchanges began to operate quickly across a range of job levels, Emily and others realized that this kind of talent redeployment—albeit at a much slower pace—will need to happen post-pandemic as economic and societal forces change the very nature of work.